# J. E. MOREN

# GOD WHO REDEEMS

ERIC H. WAHLSTROM     *Eric H. Wahlstrom*

# GOD
# WHO
# REDEEMS

*Perspectives in Biblical Theology*

MUHLENBERG PRESS          PHILADELPHIA

Dedicated

to

THE THEOLOGICAL FACULTY OF THE UNIVERSITY OF LUND, SWEDEN in grateful recognition of the honor bestowed on me as recipient of the degree of *Theologiae Doctor honoris causa* at the University Convocation in June, 1960.

# CONTENTS

# Preface

After many years as teacher of the New Testament in Augustana Theological Seminary, Rock Island, Ill., I have become increasingly aware that no one approaches the Bible without certain convictions and presuppositions. It makes a great deal of difference whether we read the Bible as history, as divine imperatives, or as a message of grace. It seems evident that in order to understand this varied and difficult collection of books which constitute our Bible, we must have a certain perspective of the whole from which we may judge and understand the different parts. This book attempts to provide such a perspective as a guide to the study of the Bible.

In its growth through my work with several generations of students, this book has become a confession, rather than a detailed study, of faith and its parts. No doubt there are inconsistencies and discrepancies in this presentation, but I am convinced that there is unity and coherence in the biblical message, even though we may be able to see it in only partial and fragmentary fashion.

It is obviously impossible to give credit to the many who during the years have enriched my life and furthered my understanding of the Bible with their insights and studies. I would like to mention especially, however, several connected with the University of Lund: Ragnar Bring, Gustaf Wingren, Hugo Odeberg, and their predecessors, Bishop Gustaf Aulén and Bishop Anders Nygren. To these men I owe a great debt of gratitude.

Special thanks are due to my colleagues, Dr. Arthur O. Arnold and Rev. Peter Beckman, who read the manuscript and made many valuable criticisms and suggestions. I also thank most cordially the editorial staff of Muhlenberg Press for their encouragement and assistance in preparing the manuscript.

E. H. W.

Pacific Lutheran Theological Seminary

Advent, 1961

# I.

# The Nature of the Bible

## INTRODUCTION

The Bible is an old and difficult book that has been the object of various interpretations. Its content is extremely diversified. It contains mythological and legendary elements,[1] historical narratives of various events, poetry, the sayings of wise men, romances, love songs, letters, prophecy, and imaginative accounts of the future. While some of its passages are unexcelled in poetic imagination, literary form, and sublimity of expression, others present rather dull accounts of names and numbers which seem to have very little to say to modern man. Some of the persons whose lives are described take their places among the great heroes of human history; others are rascals and renegades who belong among the dregs of humanity. One person is unique, and for him the book reserves a place as Lord of all in heaven and on earth. This is the Bible, a unique and remarkable collection of historical and literary material.

---

[1]Myth can be defined as "stories of gods," or stories in which gods are the actors. Since this definition is perhaps too narrow, the following one may be more satisfactory: "The mythical movement treats *on principle* all statements concerning miraculous and supernatural occurrences, especially of a direct miraculous intervention or appearance of the deity as well as any other supernatural being, on the same level. It marks them uniformly as mythical, inasmuch as the statements concerning such happenings arise from a prescientific and uncritical, naïve stage of consciousness, regardless of whether they appear in the Bible or other religious documents" (C. Hartlich and W. Sachs, *Der Ursprung des Mythosbegriffes in der modernen Bibelwissenschaft* [Tübingen, 1952], p. 148). Legends are folk stories about holy men, aiming to show the supernatural element in the life portrayed. It is not a necessary consequence of the scientific classification of myths and legends to treat them as simply fictitious stories, which lack any basis in fact or relationship to reality.

In spite of its great diversity the claim is made for this book that it has a consistent unity in all its parts: that there is a central theme from beginning to end to which the various parts are more or less loosely related. Some parts constitute the very core of the collection; other parts are so far removed from the central concern that many have suggested they might just as well have been left out. What we call the canon of Scripture has never really been settled or closed once and for all, although in our time no one will seriously suggest that any part be left out or others be admitted. The Bible stands before us in all its variety of form. In its diversity it presents its challenge to humanity, and demands an answer.

It is not strange, therefore, that the Bible has been understood in many different ways, and that the interpretations have been extremely varied. A great mass of material produced by Jewish rabbis, collected in the Talmud, interprets the Old Testament. The Jews understood the Old Testament primarily from the point of view of law. To be sure, they recognized that the Old Testament was the story of God's gracious acts in Israel, his choice of his people, and his purpose for them in the world—in other words, they recognized that they were objects of the grace of God. Nevertheless, the emphasis fell on man's duty to keep the law. The Old Testament contained the pattern of life, and the people were under obligation to observe its rules and obey its precepts. The great rabbis explained the law and tried to make it relevant to every situation in life. The Torah (i.e., the Pentateuch), which we inadequately translate as "the Law" (cf. p. 75), contained all of God's acts with Israel: his election of the chosen people, and all the other events through which he had made himself and his will known. Nevertheless, the norm according to which the interpretation was made was not God's grace but the law as commandments. The people of Israel were God's people by grace of election, but the book set forth what God demanded of them in return.

In the medieval church and in Protestant orthodoxy down to the eighteenth century the Bible was the handmaiden of dogmatics. It was regarded primarily as a depository of proof texts for the doctrines of the church. Usually these texts were taken in isolation from the context without much regard for what the original significance may have been. If law was the norm in the Jewish interpretation of the Bible, dogma was the norm in the church's interpretation. In the great struggle against Gnosticism and Marcionism the ancient church had to try to define the meaning and significance of the Old Testament for the Christian faith. Irenaeus sought to show that salvation is set in the context of a development from the Old Testament to the event of Christ: that the Old Testament represents a period of growth, development, and education, as a preparation for the act of God in Christ. In opposition to Marcion he maintained that the same God had been active in the Old Testament as in the New, although the fullness had come in Christ. Origen and the Alexandrian school resorted to allegory in their interpretation of the Old Testament. By a clever use of the "three senses of scripture," the historical, the moral, and the spiritual, they were able to discover the essential teachings of the New Testament in the Old, and thus demonstrated the unity of the Bible. The school of Antioch, however, sought to interpret the Old Testament as a historical document and to find the revelation in the acts of God. They sought to find both the historical meaning and the typological sense. They paid much attention to the text of the Old Testament and to the historical record as such.

While the initial impulse toward a critical study of the Scriptures came from the Renaissance and the Reformation, historical criticism in the eighteenth century marked a new phase in the study of biblical documents. It was now possible to subject the biblical writings to the same kind of study and criticism as any other historical documents. As a result there developed a school of the comparative study of religions, in which the religion of the Old Testament took its place alongside the religions of the other ancient Eastern peoples: the Egyptians, the Babylonians, and the Canaanites, for example. This school recognized that religion grows, that each people borrows and adapts elements from the religions of its neighbors, and that every religion represents an attempt of a people to interpret its existence and its destiny. The religion of the Old Testament was therefore considered to be inseparably connected with the fortunes and destiny of Israel. Even the New Testament message could be set in the context of the mystery religions of the Mediterranean world with their cultic rites of washings and sacral meals and their dying and rising deities. Paul was regarded as the one who had transformed the simple gospel of Jesus about the fatherhood of God and the brotherhood of man into an elaborate theological system of redemption, most of which was a combination of Hellenistic mystery religion with Jewish apocalyptic. In effect the Bible thus came to be regarded merely as part of the world's religious literature in which man has recorded his thoughts and his speculation about his gods, himself, and his destiny.

In the last three decades a new development has taken place. Greater emphasis has been placed on the uniqueness of the Old Testament and on the unity of the whole Bible. The emphasis has been shifted from man's thought about himself and his world to God's activity as it is revealed in the biblical record. The events of the Bible do not represent man's striving toward self-realization, but God's activity in judgment and redemption. Paul has expressed this in the terse statement: "God was in Christ reconciling the world to himself" (II Cor. 5:19). The human events recorded are God's acts through which he reveals himself and makes known his will. We may express the current view of the Bible by saying that the Bible is a *record* of human events, an *interpretation* of these events, and a living *message* of God to every generation.

### THE BIBLE AS A RECORD OF EVENTS IN HUMAN HISTORY

A large portion of the Bible consists of historical narratives beginning with the start of human existence and extending in prophecy into an as yet unrealized future. Although the early part of the story is obviously prehistorical, mythological, and legendary as it tells of the creation of the first human beings, the Fall, the antediluvian development, and the Flood, it is presented as fact in the form of a historical narrative of human events which provides an explanation for the later history and a setting for the subsequent development. With the beginning of the story of the patriarchs the record draws closer to actual history, and from that point onward it is substantially historical. The Bible itself, therefore, presents a historical narrative which covers the history of humanity from the beginning of existence to its consummation and final destiny. That it presents a relatively naïve and prescientific view of the world is obvious, but the historical character of the presentation is also obvious and must be recognized.

The events recorded, with the exception of creation and the final consummation, are human events. The actors are human beings, some of them all too human, and there is no attempt to give them either a superhuman or a divine stature. It is now generally agreed that the story of the wanderings of the patriarchs is actual history, perhaps embellished and expanded by tradition. The Exodus from Egypt was an actual event, and such characters as Moses, Joshua, David, and Elijah were living, historical people.

The history records all the vices and sins that continually plague humanity. There is incest, adultery, rape, murder, theft, slander, envy, treachery, pride, arrogance, cruelty, and bloodshed. All the vices enumerated by Paul in such passages as Rom. 1:29-31 and Gal. 5:19-20 can be documented in the narratives of the people of the Bible. Sometimes even those characters who form the basic links in the chain of God's chosen people, like Jacob or David, are caught in shady dealings and acts of violence. There is no attempt to hide the frailties even of the chief actors. On the other hand, the better side is also represented. There is loyalty, faithfulness, kindness, courage, and righteousness; there is fidelity, devotion to duty, and concern for the weak, the fatherless, and the widow. In short, the history of the Bible is a human history exhibiting both the glory and the degradation of man.

Like any other histories, the biblical narratives may be investigated for the purpose of ascertaining what actually happened. All the available archeological reports and historical sources other than the Bible must be examined and compared with the biblical record, not with the intention of either proving or disproving it, but simply to find the truth about the historical events. How much can be learned and checked about the Exodus and the settlement of the tribes in Canaan? How far is the record in Acts to be accepted as an accurate history of the early church? These are legitimate problems which may be investigated and the results accepted to the degree that information is available. The fact that the radical or conservative presuppositions of the investigator tend to influence his conclusions must not be used as an argument to discourage or discredit this study.

The Bible itself, as a product of human efforts, is subject to similar critical investigation. The questions of authorship, date, purpose, and significance must also be answered on the basis of critical evaluations. It is impossible to ignore the vast amount of critical biblical research produced within the past 150 years. If our conception of the Bible is such that it prevents us from asking these questions or accepting the critical results, we have to develop a new conception of the Word of God that is compatible with historical reality. The Bible is a document written by men who recorded events that occurred in human history, and as such it must submit to critical evaluation.

In our present study, however, we are not concerned with either the historical or the literary problems of the Bible. We are concerned with the Bible as it now stands, and as it is given to the church to teach and proclaim. The over-all conception of God, man, and destiny the Bible presents, within which the life of humanity is set, is intimately involved in the purpose of God as that purpose is revealed through the narrative of the Bible. In trying to set forth this conception and this purpose we must accept the whole narrative from beginning to end as in essence historical, although the creation at the beginning and the new creation at the end may be better referred to as pre- and posthistorical. The prehistory, which tells of God as Creator and of sin that enters the world as the inexplicable opposition to God, provides the setting for the human situation. The conflict is presented here, and the drama is played out in the subsequent narrative. Thus the historical record is concerned primarily with God's search for lost humanity and his struggle to overcome the hostile forces that defy his will. In the biblical view the historical narrative is the bearer of this revelation of God's will and purpose, even as it is the means through which this purpose is advanced and carried out. For this reason we take the narrative of the Bible as it stands, believing that this whole record from beginning to the end is essential for our understanding of what the biblical message has to declare to us concerning God, man, and man's destiny. Our acceptance of it as such is, in the last analysis, an act of faith.

### THE BIBLE AS AN INTERPRETATION OF THESE HISTORICAL EVENTS

The events occur in human history, but the Bible interprets them as acts of God. The Flood was not a mere natural happening: God opened the windows of heaven in order to destroy his recalcitrant people. The Exodus out of Egypt was not engineered by Moses and the enslaved people: God bared his mighty arm and led them "out of the land of Egypt, out of the house of bondage." To Cyrus, giving a few captives permission to return to their former city and rebuild their temple was no doubt a smart political move, but to the prophet who saw the return it was an act of God, who made a highway through the wilderness in order to let his people return to the land promised them and carry out his purposes. Crucifixion was a common enough event in the Mediterranean world of Jesus' time, but to Paul the Crucifixion of Jesus meant that Christ died for our sins. That Christ died is history; that it was for our sins is interpretation.

The human events in the Bible are presented to us as acts of God, through which he influences human history to destroy the powers of evil and to realize his eternal purpose. The story of the Bible is interpreted as the warfare of God against the enemies that threaten to destroy his creation. This warfare is waged in the cosmos, on the earth, and in the individual. The Bible reckons with superhuman powers: "the principalities and powers in heavenly places," "the prince of the power of the air," and "the elemental spirits of the universe." We could dismiss these expressions as ancient folklore, but—being arrayed against each other today with weapons that can exterminate us and our planet at any moment— we should still sense that behind the universe lie powers more terrible than human imagination can fathom.

The word used for "world" in the Greek scriptures is *cosmos,* which means the orderly and harmonious universe. The ancient Greeks were impressed by the orderly universe. They spoke of "the music of the spheres" and of the harmony with which the heavenly bodies move. The term "the world" in the Bible can also mean the fallen, sinful world that stands in opposition to and in enmity with the will and purpose of God. "Do not love the world" (I John 2:15). "I am not praying for the world" (John 17:9). "Now we have received not the spirit of the world" (I Cor. 2:12). "The whole world is in the power of the evil one" (I John 5:19). The world stands in opposition to God, but Jesus declares nevertheless, "I have overcome the world" (John 16:33). Just as Satan, the old serpent, must be overcome and destroyed, so the world also must die. But it must die with Christ and be transformed into the kingdom "which is not of this world" if it is not to die in the judgment which eventually will overtake all who oppose God. "For God sent the Son into the world, not to condemn the world, but that the world might be saved through him" (John 3:17).

Yet evil is found also in the individual man. The great rift between God and the forces arrayed against him is a part of man's own nature. Man is not a spectator to this cosmic conflict, he is a participant who is sometimes torn between the two opposing forces. But man, too, as separated from God and opposed to him, must die. He may be "buried with Christ by baptism into death" in order that as the new man he may "walk in newness of life" (Rom. 6:4). "The wages of sin is death" (Rom. 6:23).

The Bible interprets what happens in the world as a manifestation of the warfare of God and of his activity in judgment and redemption. It assumes the events as actual history, whether they belong to the prehistorical, legendary tradition or are near the writer's own time. It is not absolutely necessary that the record of the events be complete or even accurate. We know very little even of the life of Jesus, and still less of the events that transpired in the earlier periods. History and interpretation are so intimately intertwined that it is impossible to disentangle them. Fortunately the meaning is not dependent on the details of the event itself. Even if the Exodus did not take place exactly as recorded, it stands in Israel's history as the expression of God's mighty power and redeeming love. In spite of all the difficulties we may have with the historical record, the central conviction that God works in history to realize his purpose is expressed in every part of the biblical record.

Moreover, ultimately we have to insist that the historical record is essential. In its essence, Christianity (and Judaism) is not a philosophical, mystical, or ecstatic religion. The Bible insists that God meets man in the ordinary course of human events. The teaching of the prophets was not so much the result of mystical and ecstatic contemplation as of the prophet's personal encounter with Yahweh in the given situation of his people. The prophet discovers the character and purpose of God in the historical encounters between Yahweh and his people. God revealed his might in decisive actions, but his nature, character, and purpose could only be discovered gradually as these acts and events were interpreted in the minds of the prophets of the people.

The interpretation the prophets gave the events transformed the historical experience of a people, which belongs to a certain time and place, into something which applies to the universal history of humanity. The Exodus occurred at a certain time and place, but it says to all mankind that God is the one who constantly redeems and gives life. The event of Christ took place in Palestine in the first century, but the meaning of the event is salvation for the world. These events are acts of God, and become, therefore, a part of his eternal and universal purpose.

The interpretation is inseparable from the event. Nor can the event be discarded after the interpretation has been apprehended. The meaning and significance of the Lord's Supper cannot be separated from the event that took place in the upper room "on the night when he was betrayed." No matter how much the rite may be changed and developed within the church, it is inseparably connected with the action and the words of the Lord on that occasion. Separated from that event it becomes a mystery cult without roots in historical reality. The biblical record and the interpretation must be held together, because it is through these historical events that God acts and makes known his character and purpose.

## THE BIBLE AS A MESSAGE OF GOD TO EVERY GENERATION

Both the record of a biblical event and the interpretation of it belong to the past, and in that light have little significance for man today. Why should modern man be interested in the wanderings of the patriarchs, or the vicissitudes of Israel's history, or even in the life and death of Jesus? All those events belong to the distant past, and they are relatively unimportant compared to other great events in the history of mankind. Are the biblical events still relevant for a man living in the modern space age and facing the problems of an entirely different environment and civilization?

If we let the Bible itself answer our question, the answer is twofold.[2] The Bible is still relevant because neither God nor man has changed. First, God's situation is always the same. God contends against the same enemies—the devil, the world, and the flesh—in all ages from Genesis to Revelation. The battle front shifts and the circumstances vary, but the action is always the same. There is no doubt in the Bible that God is supreme at all times, that the course of history moves according to his plan, and that he will ultimately triumph. For his own inscrutable reasons he does not at once destroy his enemies. He works according to his own plan. The warfare is continuous until the final consummation.

---

[2]Cf. Gustaf Wingren, *The Living Word,* trans. Victor C. Pogue (Philadelphia, 1960), p. 46.

In this sense, God's situation will be the same as long as this world lasts.

Second, man's situation in relation to God is always the same. He is a sinner and a rebel, a slave under alien powers, who is opposed to God's will and hostile to his government. All men in every generation are separated from God, lost and perishing. Man, too, must be overcome and his hostility removed. He must be brought to a surrender to God's will. Because man is always a sinner in need of forgiveness, and God is always the only one who can redeem and give life, the proclamation of God's redemptive activity in the past is relevant to every generation.

Thus the story of Abraham, for example, is not just ancient history. It affirms that what God did with Abraham he can also do now in bringing man out of his sinful native habitat to "the land that I will show you." Bishop Nygren has made use of the following analogy to set forth this effective character of the Word of God.[3] Toward the end of the Second World War a message went out to the occupied countries of Europe: "The enemy has been defeated! Norway is free! Denmark is free!" An event had taken place on the continent which changed the situation for every man, woman, and child in these two countries. The proclamation of the message set men free. They could come out from their hiding places and breathe again the clean air of freedom. The event and the proclamation were objective realities, and the man who believed the message, acted on it, and came out from underground found that it was true. For him it was effective, but for anyone who did not believe the news, bondage remained. In the same manner, says Nygren, the event of Christ has taken place as an objective reality, the victory has been won, and the proclamation of the event means freedom for those who hear and believe. The Bible is that living, active, and effective proclamation.

Unlike the Norwegians and the Danes, sinners need not wait for news from the continent. God's action is not confined to an

[3]Anders Nygren, *The Gospel of God*, trans. L. J. Trinterud (Philadelphia, 1951), pp. 29-30.

engagement at a single time and place. In his warfare against his enemies the battle occurs all along the line, and he is present everywhere to redeem his people and set them free. The Word of God, therefore, is not merely a report about something that has happened elsewhere or in the past: it is God's activity *now* in the present generation. The past events reveal what God is doing now through his word: he redeems and gives life.

When we speak of the Word of God as living and active, we are using "word" in a different sense from the modern popular usage. A word is usually thought of as imparting information, and the idea of action is not immediately apparent. In speaking of the Bible as God's word to men, we may, therefore, create the impression that the Word of God is primarily supposed to furnish information about man's life and destiny. Man is ignorant of his true nature, but God speaks, and then man is informed. This would make man's dilemma ignorance rather than sin, and his salvation a matter of acquiring knowledge rather than finding redemption. In the language of the Bible, however, "word" has a much more active meaning than it has in modern English. "By the word of the Lord were the heavens made" (Ps. 33: 6 A.V.). At times the authors of the Bible even seem to have thought of God's word as a power or agency more or less distinct from God. In the Bible, "word" is a means of communication and *action*. God's word is creative of new realities (see, for example, Isa. 55: 10-11 and Matt. 8:16), and God speaks through his acts. We should not say, "God *speaks* and reveals himself," but rather, "God *acts* and reveals himself."

John's Gospel speaks of Christ as the Word, and many would prefer to say that ultimately he is *the* Word. This is profoundly true, provided Christ is not understood in a narrow sense as referring only to the Incarnation or the event of the Cross and the Resurrection. Christ is always the agent of God in creation, providence, and redemption (John 1:1-3; Col. 1:16-17; Heb. 1:2). Even the final redemption and the new creation will be his work. He is the living Lord who is now present and active in the world to do the same redemptive work that is recorded in the Bible in the stories of Abraham and of the Exodus, and in the Gospels. In this wider sense it is true that Christ is the Word, and "the Word became flesh and dwelt among us" (John 1:14). His presence and activity make the biblical Word a living, redemptive message to men in every generation.

## REFORMATION PRINCIPLES AND THE BIBLE

The Protestant Reformation emphasized two principles which have a bearing on our conception of the Bible. The formal principle declared that Holy Scripture is the sole rule of faith and life, and the material principle is stated in the doctrine of justification by grace through faith.

### The Formal Principle

The confessions of faith declare that "the Word of God shall establish articles of faith, and no one else, not even an angel."[4] The introduction to the Formula of Concord declares: "We believe, teach, and confess that the prophetic and apostolic writings of the Old and New Testaments are the only rule and norm according to which all doctrines and teachers alike must be appraised and judged . . ."[5] This principle was directed against the Roman Catholic contention that the tradition of the church and the pronouncements of popes and councils were on a par with Scripture. The Reformers made a clear distinction between Holy Scripture and any other writings, and professed to recognize Scripture alone as judge, rule and norm by which all teachings and all teachers had to be examined to judge whether they were good or bad, true or false. This principle is still to be taken seriously, we feel, but their formulation of it and the emphasis they gave it must be understood in the light of the conflict situation in which the men of the Reformation stood, if we are to avoid the dangers of funda-

---

[4]*The Book of Concord,* trans. and ed. Theodore G. Tappert (Philadelphia, 1959), p. 295.
[5]*Ibid.,* p. 464.

mentalism and legalism that lie in accepting the formal principle
without the material one.

If all doctrines and teachings are to be derived and deduced
from Scripture, the result is that the biblical statements are taken as
timeless truths without reference to the original situation or the
situation of today. On this principle the Bible becomes a servant
of dogmatics, and its material is used as proof texts. This procedure
is possible only on the assumption that the biblical word is inerrant and perfect in every detail and uniformly authoritative. The
biblical record is assumed to be a depository of timeless truths
which can be lifted out of their context and incorporated into a
theological system.

When the Bible is regarded as the sole rule of life and conduct,
it becomes a legal code which is made to apply to all the circumstances and situations in life. Again its statements are lifted out
of their context, and its precepts are interpreted as timeless rules
which apply everywhere and for all time. Of course, no one has
ever succeeded in carrying out such an interpretation in all its
details. The lawyers and the scribes of Jesus' day tried to make the
commandments applicable to all the circumstances of life, explaining them in such a way that with reasonable efforts they could be
obeyed. But in spite of the assumed timelessness of the rules, times
change and new interpretations must be made. The acceptance of
the formal principle by itself, the principle that the Scriptures are
the sole rule of faith and life, makes the Bible a legal code which
petrifies the Word into lifeless dogmas and oppressive rules which
frequently become irrelevant to real life.

*The Material Principle*

If these errors are to be avoided, the formal principle must
be interpreted and applied in the light of the material principle of
justification by grace through faith. The doctrine of justification,
the Apology of the Augsburg Confession states, is "the main doctrine of Christianity . . . when it is properly understood, it illu-

mines and magnifies the honor of Christ."[6] A German variant here adds this significant statement: "[Justification by faith] is of especial service for the clear, correct understanding of the entire Holy Scriptures, and alone shows the way to the unspeakable treasures and right knowledge of Christ, and alone opens the door to the entire Bible."[7] The Bible must be understood from its central message that God is the Creator and Redeemer who by his gracious acts saves man and gives him life. The Bible is a record of God's creative and redemptive activity until the final consumation. The message of the whole Bible is that God comes into the world to save sinners and to restore them to fellowship with himself.

It may be said that the center of the Bible is Christ, keeping in mind that Christ must also be understood as the Alpha and the Omega: the one who acts at all times as the agent of God's redemptive activity. In this sense Luther could say: "Whatever does not teach Christ is not yet apostolic, even though St. Peter or St. Paul does the teaching. Again, whatever preaches Christ would be apostolic, even if Judas, Annas, Pilate, and Herod were doing it."[8]

The material principle stands guard against all legalistic, dogmatic, capricious, or individualistic interpretations of the Bible. It demands that we read the Bible in the light of its central message of the grace of God, and that we relate every part of the Bible to this central theme. Understood from this center, the Bible does become the sure and sole rule of faith and life. It is not possible then to pick and choose that which appeals to us, or what *we* may regard as central and meaningful. We must allow the Bible to be what it is in all its parts: a message of God's redemptive activity in human history.

It was the material principle that enabled Luther at once to criticize certain aspects of the Bible and to claim that he was entirely bound by Scripture. He criticized Hebrews for teaching that

---

[6] *Ibid.,* p. 107.
[7] *The Book of Concord,* ed. Henry E. Jacobs (Philadelphia, 1882), I, 84.
[8] *Word and Sacrament I,* ed. E. Theodore Bachmann, genl. ed. Helmut T. Lehmann ("Luther's Works," Vol. XXXV [55 vols.; Philadelphia, 1960]), p. 396.

there is no second repentance (Heb. 6:4-6),[9] and he called James "an epistle of straw."[10] He suggested that some books like Esther, Song of Solomon, James, II Peter, Jude and Revelation might as well have been left out of the canon. Of the prophets he said that in their preaching of Christ they did not err, but when they declared something about kings and historical events, as they sometimes did, they were frequently mistaken.[11] On the other hand, Luther insisted that Scripture was the norm by which his own teaching and that of his adversaries must be judged. He insisted that the very wording of the text had to be observed and accepted just as it stood. His conception of the Bible was such that he could be at the same time most free and most securely captive.

The key to Luther's attitude to the Bible is to be found in the fact that he had discovered its central message. In his early life his chief concern had been the word of Scripture in a general and formal sense, but after he had received his new insight into the nature of Scripture, it was the word of grace *(das Gnadenwort),* the message of a gracious and forgiving God, which became the real object of his faith. He read the Bible in the conviction that it was nothing else but the great message that God is gracious toward men: that he operates in history and in Christ to redeem them from sin and death "purely out of fatherly and divine goodness and mercy, without any merit or worthiness in [us]."[12] When the Bible is understood in this sense, we can allow for historical and literary criticism and yet hold to the letter of Scripture and the authority of its message.

## THE BIBLE AS AUTHORITY FOR FAITH

The Reformation made three affirmations of exclusive character: *sola scriptura, sola gratia,* and *sola fide.* We have already suggested that the first of these must be understood in the light of the second and third. It is, therefore, questionable whether it can be categori-

---

[9]*Ibid.,* p. 394.     [10]*Ibid.,* p. 362.
[11]*D. Martin Luther's sämmtliche Werke,* ed. E. L. Enders (2d ed.; Frankfurt, 1867), VIII, 23.
[12]*Dr. Martin Luther's Small Catechism* (Rock Island, Ill., 1941), p. 11.

cally stated that we accept the Bible *alone* as authority. The Reformers were opposed to the emphasis on tradition and the authority of the church, but this opposition led them to a greater emphasis
on the Bible *alone* than can reasonably be maintained. Scripture
as authority for faith must be considered in the context of two other
factors: the church (tradition) and the living Spirit.

All of us read the Bible in the light of the teaching of the church
in which we have been reared. Just as most Lutherans have been
nurtured on the basis of Luther's Catechisms, some members of the
Reformed tradition have been on the Heidelberg Catechism, and
Anglicans on the Book of Common Prayer. Such diverse and numerous traditions as the Greek Orthodox, Roman Catholic, Lutheran, Baptist, Methodist, Presbyterian, and others determine to
some extent our understanding of the Bible. The fact that two di-
vergent views on baptism both appeal to the Bible for authority
could indicate something beside the biblical word is involved. It is
futile to claim that any of us comes to the Bible with a completely
open mind. Not even the scholar is able to recognize and discount
his presuppositions entirely. That Lutherans have accepted justification by faith as a guide to understanding the Bible is largely due
to the tradition in which they stand.

Not only is it impossible to ignore tradition, it would be foolish
to do so. We must pay attention to what the church has taught in
these two thousand years, how it has understood the biblical message, and how it has experienced the grace of God in Christ. In
doing so we must make allowance for the historical situation in any
age. The feudal system of the Middle Ages influenced the interpretation of the Bible, and the social structure of Luther's day is reflected in his writings. At the present time there are those who
claim that the democratic ideals of the Western world most closely
approximate the spirit of the Bible, or at least of the New Testament, with respect to social organization.[13] Every age reads the

---

[13]John Wick Bowman, *Prophetic Realism and the Gospel* (Philadelphia,
1955), pp. 267-8. Cf. Karl Barth, "Christengemeinde und Bürgergemeinde,"
*Theologische Studien* (1946), p. 36. "There is an affinity between the Christian
community and the civic community of the free peoples."

Bible in the light of its own peculiar problems. For this very reason, the teaching of the church both in the past and in the present must be taken into consideration. The authority is not *sola scriptura,* but Scripture as interpreted and understood in the tradition and life of the church. The Bible is the *living* word of God, and as such it is always involved in the thought and culture of every age.

The other factor which must be taken into consideration is the living Spirit. Jesus promised to send his Spirit, who was to "teach you all things, and bring to your remembrance all that I have said to you" (John 14:26). If we believe in the reality of the presence of the risen Lord and the living Spirit within the faithful, we must also believe in the continual guidance of the Spirit. The Spirit illumines, enlightening the believer and applying the biblical word to his situation. It is undeniable that in the course of time the Spirit has led men into new truth and a wider understanding of the biblical word.

All three factors—Bible, church and Spirit—must be taken into consideration in our understanding of the biblical message. If one factor is emphasized to the virtual exclusion of the other, the result is error. When the Bible itself is made the sole rule, the result is fundamentalism and legalism. When the church becomes supreme, the result is hierarchical tyranny and suppression of truth. When the Spirit is regarded as operating independently, the result is unbridled individualism and confusion. Only in the combination of the Bible, the church, and the living Spirit can we find the true guide and adequate authority for faith. We must add, however, that in this combination the Bible retains the primary authority as the unchanging witness to God's acts in history. The teaching of the church and the testimony of the Spirit must be tested ultimately by agreement with the message of Scripture. But it is then Scripture as understood in the context of the church and under the guidance of the Spirit.

The Bible thus understood and interpreted is the Word of God. This means the whole Bible as we have it now in English or in any other language, not just the original. If only the autographs could be regarded as really the inspired Word of God, the church would exist without an authentic Word of God. Since the autographs are lost, we do not have the means to determine with certainty how far the present-day text is removed from the original. We may regret the loss, but it is not a threat to the faith of the church. The Bible which we now have—in any English version that is a fairly accurate translation from any reasonably good Hebrew and Greek text—is the Bible which God has given us. The vast majority of people have no other Word of God. We must take this Word as it stands with all the marks of imperfection and all the variations between the different accounts. It would be presumptuous to demand that God should have given us a different book, one that was historically accurate, grammatically perfect and unmistakably divine. It does not help matters to say that God has given us such a book, but that he has permitted it to become changed and mutilated in transmitting it from one copy to another. The acceptance of this book as the Word of God is under any circumstances an act of faith, and we have to take it, therefore, just as it is: as God has given it to us.

The demand for a divine and inerrant book represents the ancient heresy of Docetism, which refused to recognize the true humanity of our Lord. Man always seeks to eliminate the finite elements in his hold on the divine. The result may be a Savior who is a wholly divine person, the transubstantiated elements of the Lord's Supper, the pure and divine church, or the inerrant and perfect book. All of these attempt to enhance the divine at the expense of the human and to provide man with a spurious miracle as a basis for faith. But God's word comes to us incarnate in a human book, as in the incarnate Christ. The words are human words, the words of men who had received the Spirit of God, and who were used as his instruments and messengers. We have to take these words exactly as they stand and pay attention even to the variations in the text and the apparent discrepancies. The only way we can get the message is by reading the words and trying to understand them in their historical context and in the light of the central message of salvation by grace through faith. The truly human and truly divine Bible is the living and active Word of God which constitutes the authority for faith and life.

# 2.

# The Decisive Events of the Bible

### THE LIVING AND ACTIVE GOD

The Bible begins in eternity and ends in eternity. It begins with God and ends with God. "In the beginning God created the heavens and the earth." "In the beginning was the Word." "It is done! I am the Alpha and the Omega, the beginning and the end." Between these two extremes lies the history of God's dealings with humanity and his activity on behalf of his creation. The Bible is primarily the story of God: his will, his activity, and his purpose. It is the history of God's approach to man, and of man's response to God's impingement upon his existence.

The God of the Bible is the living and active God. The sense of God's nearness and of his immediate relationship to his creation is expressed throughout the Bible, sometimes in naïve, simple, and anthropomorphic terms. God walks in the garden in the cool of the day, he instructs Noah how to build the ark, he talks with the patriarchs, and he himself fights the battles of his people. Jesus sees the evidence of the heavenly Father's care in the brilliant colors of the flowers and in the sustenance given to the birds of the air. Especially does God care for those who trust in him. Jesus tells his disciples: "Even the hairs of your head are all numbered." God lives and works in his creative and redemptive activity, in his providential care for his creation, and in his personal relationship with men. Though he is high and holy, and his throne is in heaven, he is still near his creatures and concerned with their circumstances

21

and destiny. "I have seen the affliction of my people who are in Egypt, and I have heard their cry because of their taskmasters; I know their sufferings, and I have come down to deliver them."

Over against the biblical emphasis on God as living, active, and present is man's natural tendency to remove God as far as possible from everyday life, while keeping him near enough to call on in emergencies. Even Confucius said: "Treat the gods with respect, but keep them at a distance." To keep God at a distance may be dictated by man's desire to enhance and exalt the majesty and glory of a God who dwells in light unapproachable, but it may also serve to make man feel independent, and supposedly escape close supervision by an unseen power.

In the Judaism contemporary with Jesus and Paul, the law had largely taken the place of the immediate presence of God. God had been active in the past—in the Exodus, in the prophets, and in the return from the Exile—and he would again some day bare his strong arm, redeem his people from bondage, and pour upon them his Spirit. For the present, he had given them a sacred book, a code of law, which was to govern their lives and their relationship to him. If they would listen to the law and comply reasonably well with its precepts, they could expect his favor and his blessing. Of course, the law had to be interpreted reasonably so that it could be obeyed. When thus interpreted it could serve as a shield against too radical demands of God in the present. A man could say: "All these I have kept from my youth."

Even the church has sometimes lost the New Testament sense of the presence of God. The Bible, regarded merely as a record of what God has spoken in the *past,* can be misused as a shield for man against too close a contact with God. If God has spoken a Word that is finished and recorded in a book, then he can be held to his Word, runs a popular sophistry. He cannot speak anything more or new. He becomes the God who *spoke* instead of the *Deus loquens,* the God who speaks *now* directly to man in his present situation. Man can "claim the promises" as long as he complies with what God has stated in the code. In this school of thought, the Bible comes to stand between man and God, and man achieves an unwarranted sense of autonomy from God.

In contrast, the New Testament is filled with the consciousness of God's immediate presence and activity. The Holy Spirit is poured out on the believer. God directs the missionary activity of the church. Jesus promises his disciples: "I am with you always, to the close of the age" (Matt. 28:20). Paul's most characteristic expression for the Christian life is "in Christ": "I have been crucified with Christ; it is no longer I who live, but Christ who lives in me" (Gal. 2:20). Paul claims to have worked harder in the proclamation of the gospel than anyone else, "though it was not I, but the grace of God which is with me" (I Cor. 15:10). He looks at his small mission congregations and declares: "You are God's field, God's building" (I Cor. 3:9). God is at work in the congregation as a farmer in his field or a builder in a house. The New Testament continues and maintains the same conception of the living and active God as is found in the Old Testament, where the narratives present God as the maker of the history of his people, the prophets who interpret the events declare God's judgment and redemption, and the psalmists celebrate the creative, redemptive, and providential activity of the Lord.

This constant activity of God is directed and controlled by his eternal purpose. He does not move in circles, nor does he simply keep things going in their accustomed order. The biblical narrative presents God as having a definite plan, which he unfolds and reveals to men. God's plan had its inception in the mystery of the mind of God "before the foundation of the world" (Eph. 1:4). Paul, especially, celebrates the purpose of God. He declares that we have been destined, chosen and appointed in Christ "according to the purpose of him who accomplishes all things according to the counsel of his will" (1:11). The mystery of God's will and purpose is made known to us in Christ. This eternal purpose is concerned with the destiny of humanity and especially with those persons who "have been destined and appointed to live for the praise of his glory" (1:12).

The goal of this purposive activity of God is stated in various ways. Negatively, it implies the overthrow of the powers of Satan and a triumph over all the principalities and powers that oppose God. Evil powers having entered his creation and threatened to destroy it, God's activity becomes a conflict with them. The devil shall be thrown into the lake of fire, and the last enemy, death, shall be destroyed. Positively, the goal is redemption of God's people: salvation and life in the presence of God. The ultimate goal is to redeem man, to rescue creation from death and destruction, and to establish the everlasting kingdom. The Bible both presents the conflict realistically and reveals to man the ultimate goal toward which God's whole creation moves. For a right understanding of the Bible it is necessary to take seriously the facts of the creation, the Fall, the redemptive conflict, and the ultimate goal of God's purpose. God is dealing with a humanity that he created, but a humanity that has fallen into sin and stands in opposition to his will. The Bible is concerned from beginning to end with what God has done, is doing, and will do to redeem humanity and to realize his eternal purpose.

## THE SEVEN BIBLICAL EVENTS

The Bible records God's activity: his dealings with Israel and humanity. It is he who acts in history. The narratives are written from the point of view that God is the acting subject and man is the passive object. God provides for the salvation of Noah; he calls Abraham; he leads the people out of Egypt and establishes them in the promised land. The subsequent history of Israel is governed by the purpose and activity of God. He makes and directs its history. Its conflicts are not only Israel's wars with its enemies, but also, the Israelites being his chosen people, the wars of the Lord. A book cited as a source in Num. 21:14 is entitled "The Book of the Wars of the Lord." In the New Testament, "God was in Christ reconciling the world to himself." In the final scene to which the New Testament looks forward, "the tabernacle of God is with men . . .

God shall wipe away all tears" and he who sits on the great white throne declares: "Behold, I make all things new."

The prophets and especially the psalmists celebrate the glory and majesty of God's works:

> The heavens are telling the glory of God; and the firmament proclaims his handiwork.
>
> The Mighty One, God the Lord, speaks and summons the earth from the rising of the sun to its setting.
>
> Come and see what God has done: he is terrible in his deeds among men.
>
> At thy rebuke, O God of Jacob, both rider and horse lay stunned.
>
> *—Ps. 19:1, 50:1, 66:5, 76:6*

Perhaps the most eloquent description of God's majesty and power in action is that found in chapter 40 of Isaiah. Similar examples in the New Testament are the hymns in Luke: the Magnificat (1:46-55), the Benedictus (1:68-79), and the Nunc Dimittis (2:29-32). The hymns in Revelation have the same theme. It is significant that this theme occurs so frequently in poetic form, for it is their hymns and songs that express the deepest faith and devotion of a people. It is evident that the biblical faith in a living and active God was deeply rooted in the consciousness of the faithful in Israel. The subject of their praise is the wonderful works of God.

While the whole Bible is concerned with setting forth the purposeful and continuous activity of God, his activity is seen most clearly and significantly in a certain series of events which highlights the narrative. God is active at all times, but at certain critical points he invades human history in a special way. To select among the many such events may seem subjective and arbitrary, but the Bible itself indicates the importance of certain events by the amount of narrative and interpretation devoted to them.

In the biblical history seven great events seem to constitute the essential content of the Bible and the core of God's revelation of himself. They are the Fall, the Flood, the call of Abraham, the

Exodus, the return from the Exile, the life of Christ, and the Parousia. All these are acts of God, events in which he comes to men and gives a new direction to man's history and opens a new stage in his situation. These events in which God deals with the fallen creation and sinful humanity constitute the theme of the biblical revelation. We cannot count creation among these events of "history," since this act stands at the beginning and provides the scene on which the historical drama is played out. The biblical history is concerned with the conflict which begins as sin enters the creation which God pronounced good, and it continues until this creation is restored and God's eternal purpose is fulfilled.

In the event described as occurring in Eden we are concerned, therefore, with the story of God's coming to this first pair of human beings after they had disobeyed the commandment and fallen into sin. This story, like the story of Noah, is mythical, poetic, and couched in anthropomorphic language, and appeared in the biblical record at a relatively late date. We are not concerned here with the question of the origin and the development of the Old Testament material. Our purpose is to interpret the biblical record as it has been given to us, looking back from the vantage point of later history upon the whole series of events in the revelation of God. The significance of these events for us is not to be found in their historicity as such, but rather in what they reveal about God's approach to man and about the purpose and destiny of his creation. It will become apparent that all these events contain some of the same elements and have similar meaning and significance for the relationship between God and man.

When Adam and Eve disobeyed God and became subject to sin, death, and the devil, God came to them. His coming brought judgment upon the sinners. He pronounced a curse upon the serpent and the ground itself, but he did not abandon the rebellious human beings to death. The very fact that he came to them constitutes an act of redemption. Although it had been said that "in the day that you eat of it you shall die" (Gen. 2:17), God's coming to them and his call to them meant the possibility of redemption and life.

The story has a naïve guise: God walked in the garden in the cool of the day seeking for his wayward children. "The Lord God called to the man, and said to him, 'where are you?'" (Gen. 3:9). Yet Jesus did not really add anything more in his parables of the lost sheep and the lost coin than what this simple narrative in Genesis had already said—God goes out to seek and to save the lost. His coming also involved a promise, expressed in terms of man's "bruising" the serpent's head. As far as the biblical record is concerned the struggle between God and the demonic forces that have enslaved humanity begins at the Fall; in other words, that event was the beginning of the redemptive activity of God. In the realism of the biblical record his coming was not simply a promise of something that he would do in the future, it was a redemptive act whereby God at that moment judged and redeemed his creation. The Fall is the beginning of the *Heilsgeschichte,* the history of redemption, and each subsequent event is a link in the process which leads to the final consummation.

In each subsequent event these three factors—judgment, redemption, and promise—are present. The Flood was the judgment of God upon the antediluvian people, but Noah and his house were saved, and the promise given to man before the Fall that he should possess the earth was repeated to him. God called Abraham out of the heathen environment of Mesopotamia. This call involved judgment on the present setting of his existence and was an act of redemption. "Abraham believed God, and it was reckoned to him as righteousness" (Rom. 4:3). To this Abraham who believed the promise was given. In the other four events—the Exodus, the Exile, Christ, the Parousia—these three elements of judgment, redemption, and promise are obvious.

The presence of these factors gives the biblical events their peculiar character and significance. This is God's approach to man. Since man is a sinner, God's coming inevitably means a judgment on his sinfulness and disobedience. God's judgment, however, is not simply vengeance and destruction, but a part of God's government of the world. His coming and his presence with men provides the

possibility of redemption for those who hear his call and obey his
will. He comes not only to judge but to redeem. Yet this redemption cannot mean anything unless there is also a promise for the
future, a promise that "he who began a good work in you will
bring it to completion at the day of Jesus Christ" (Phil. 1:6).
Whenever God comes to man, all three factors are always present.
The significance of his coming into the world is illustrated and veri-
fied by the events in the biblical record; thus the Bible reveals God
as Judge, Redeemer, and ultimate Victor.

It might be argued that instead of concentrating on these events
we should interpret the biblical record in terms of the covenants
between God and men. This suggestion lies close at hand since we
are accustomed to speak of the Old and the New Testaments or
Covenants, but the word covenant does not adequately express the
relationship between God and man to us. It inevitably suggests to
us a pact between two independent parties who negotiate and bind
themselves to the terms of the covenant. Moreover, the thought of
a "covenant" easily assumes legalistic connotations which obscure
the fact that it is God who in grace and mercy enters into fellowship with man. It is God who takes the initiative and comes to man.
His coming and activity is the prerequisite for the covenant and the
basis of it.[1] God saved Noah, and then established his covenant with
him. Abraham was called and he obeyed; then the covenant was
instituted. God redeemed his people out of slavery in Egypt, and
with this redeemed people, his people, he entered into the covenant at Mount Sinai. The preamble of that covenant said: "I am
the Lord your God, who brought you out of the land of Egypt, out
of the house of bondage," therefore, "You shall have no other gods
before me" (Exod. 20:2-3). First the relationship to God was established by his act of redemption, and then God made his will
known to his people in the terms of the covenant. The new cove-

---

[1] G. Ernest Wright states: "Election [the event] is more primary in Israel than
covenant. While the two go together, the latter is a conceptual language for ex-
pressing the meaning of the former and it makes considerable difference as to
which receives the primary emphasis" (*God Who Acts* [Chicago, 1952], p. 36,
n. 1).

nant, too, was established "in the blood of Christ." The redemptive event comes first and constitutes the foundation on which the covenant is made.

The word event emphasizes that the relationship to God is based on grace, while the word covenant can easily suggest that the relationship is predicated on man's effort to fulfill the law. Millar Burrows states:

> The conditions of the divine favor on which all human welfare depends are stated in a series of covenants, beginning with one for all the descendants of Noah, continuing with successive covenants between God and the patriarchs, and culminating in the great covenant with Israel at Mount Sinai . . . Since a contract involves the assumption of definite obligations, the covenant between God and Israel necessitated a specific statement of what God promised and also of what he required of Israel.[2]

The description is no doubt correct, and Burrows does note that it is God who takes the initiative in establishing the covenant. Nevertheless the emphasis seems to fall on "God's requirements," and the fact that in each case the covenant is preceded by a redemptive act of God tends to be obscured. Again we must remember the preamble of the covenant at Mount Sinai. It was the redemption of the Israelites out of Egypt that made them God's people, as is amply evidenced by the emphasis the prophets and psalmists place upon the Exodus. To this redeemed people God makes known his will and gives directions for their lives. Because they are his redeemed people, their response to him should not be matter of legal compulsion but of spontaneous desire to do his will. It is not a matter simply of a contractual obligation, but of a fellowship in obedience and faith.

It is perhaps necessary to justify the inclusion of the return from the Exile as one of these great biblical events. It might seem that it was rather a minor event, since the glories that had once attended the great era of David and Solomon never returned. When the foundation of the temple was laid, many of the priests and Levites and other men who had seen the first temple "wept with a loud

---

[2]Millar Burrows, *An Outline of Biblical Theology* (Philadelphia, 1946), p. 11.

voice," so that the people could not distinguish between the sound of rejoicing and weeping (Ezra 3:12). Except for a brief period of freedom under the Maccabean princes the people remained in bondage to foreign powers, and the promise of a new era remained a promise and a hope. However, it is not the greatness of the event in terms of worldly power, but its meaning that is important. The interpretation of this event must not be derived only from the books of Ezra and Nehemiah. Its meaning is revealed rather in the prophecies of second Isaiah and Jeremiah. It is evident that chapters 40–66 of Isaiah represent the vision of the prophet as he ponders the meaning of this return to Jerusalem which is now assured through the generosity of Cyrus. Whatever interpretation may be given to the details and to the mysterious person of the Suffering Servant, it cannot be denied that the vision refers to the return from the Exile. The very mention of Cyrus as the Anointed of the Lord is sufficient proof of this.

The prophet sees in the return of the exiles the beginning of a great and magnificent era. God prepares a way for his people to return home. "In the wilderness" (that separated the exiles from Jerusalem) "prepare the way of the Lord, make straight in the desert a highway for our God" (Isa. 40:3). Now the eschatological hour has come, now "the glory of the Lord shall be revealed, and all flesh shall see it together, for the mouth of the Lord has spoken" (Isa. 40:5). Now the promise made to Abraham shall at last be fulfilled, and Israel will receive a blessing and be a blessing to "all the families of the earth" (Gen. 12:3). This nation which now returns shall be a holy nation, a kingdom of priests, a people for God's own possession. Now God will give Israel as "a light to the nations, that my salvation may reach to the end of the earth" (Isa. 49:6). "All the ends of the earth shall see the salvation of our God" (Isa. 52:10). The nations shall hear the gospel of the living God and shall come to the "holy mountain, . . . for my house shall be called a house of prayer *for all peoples*" (Isa. 56:7) (italics added). Zion and Jerusalem shall be the center from which the salvation of God shall reach all the earth. This is not a vision of some far-away, distant event; this is what the prophet expects will happen *now* as the exiles return to their native land.

Jeremiah, the other prophet who deals with the Exile, sees the return in less universal terms. He is concerned primarily with the restoration of Israel. He wrote earlier than second Isaiah, but like Isaiah he interprets the return as the beginning of a new era. The new covenant which God will now establish with his people will be greater than that made with the fathers who were redeemed out of Egypt. In this new covenant, says the Lord, "I will put my law within them, and I will write it upon their hearts; and I will be their God, and they shall be my people." Then all Israel will know the Lord, and he will "forgive their iniquity and . . . remember their sin no more" (Jer. 31:31 ff.).

Could the prophets really have believed that the return of a few exiles was the great event through which God would establish his kingdom? We know, of course, from Ezra and Nehemiah, that the returning exiles were few and that the actual history had nothing of the grandeur we find in the vision of the prophets. But we need only recall another even smaller group of humble Galilean fishermen who made the astounding claim that an obscure teacher who had been condemned and hanged on a cross was the exalted Lord of heaven and earth and that in his name alone was there salvation and life. The prophets of the Exile who interpreted the event *believed in God.* They did not look at the small number of the people, they looked to the eternal God. Their cry was: "Behold your God! Behold, the Lord comes with might, and his arm rules for him" (Isa. 40:10). "Behold, the nations are like a drop from a bucket, and are accounted as the dust on the scales" (40:15). "Fear not, you worm Jacob, you men of Israel! I will help you, says the Lord; your redeemer is the Holy One of Israel" (41:14). The prophets did not look at the exiles, but to this God of Israel who now was to manifest his power and establish his kingdom.

We may suggest two reasons why the return from the Exile has not been recognized in the eschatological light in which the prophets understood it. In the first place, the vision of the great prophet did not materialize. What actually happened is recorded in Ezra and Nehemiah. The exiles refused to accept the challenge of universality and concentrated on themselves. They refused the role of the Suffering Servant. Instead of universalism they followed the line of intense nationalism and isolationism. They said, we are God's people and we must separate ourselves from the world. We must build a wall around ourselves and guard our treasure. They did so with the good intention of keeping themselves free of heathen pollution, but they had not learned the difficult lesson that "whoever would save his life will lose it; and whoever loses his life for my sake, he will save it" (Luke 9:24).

In the second place, the prophecies of Isaiah and Jeremiah have been interpreted so exclusively with reference to the New Testament that their reference to the return from the Exile has been ignored. The voice in the wilderness is John the Baptist, the Suffering Servant is Jesus, and the new covenant is the New Testament. However much truth there may be in this interpretation, it must not be forgotten that the prophets saw in the event of their times a great redemptive act of God, through which a new age would dawn for God's people and for the world. The prophets were not speaking of the distant future but of the *immediate* future. *Now* "the time is fulfilled, the kingdom of God is at hand. Prepare the way of the Lord."

The returning exiles rejected the great vision of their prophets. The great promise, "by you all the families of the earth will bless themselves," was not fulfilled this time. The same challenge was to be made later by a greater One than even the unknown prophet of the Exile, and his appeal, too, would be rejected. Lest we judge too harshly, let us remember that even in the Christian church we have been satisfied to enjoy the distinction of being God's people without showing much concern for the multitudes of humanity who "sit in darkness and the shadow of death." The challenge to become the Suffering Servant of the Lord is never easy to accept.

The biblical perspective is seen and expressed in this series of redemptive events. Although the selection of these seven events may seem arbitrary, it can hardly be denied that they are the great events in this record of God's dealings with men. They are decisive in the history of salvation. Man has fallen into sin, he has become separated from God, and he is now the slave of demonic powers. He is "dead in trespasses and sins, without God and without hope in the world." This situation is changed when God comes into the world in judgment and redemption. God works according to his eternal purpose, and these events are his mighty acts in history through which this purpose is revealed and realized. "God moves in a mysterious way his wonders to perform."

From the perspective of these redemptive events there is an essential unity in the Bible. This unity does not consist in human history, or in man's response, or even in man's interpretation of these events. The return from the Exile could be interpreted as a universal gospel for all peoples, but it could also be interpreted as an opportunity to establish an exclusive and privileged people whom God had selected as his own. In the New Testament the event of Christ could be interpreted as the giving of a new law (Matthew), the bestowal of eternal life (John), justification by faith (Paul), or the fulfillment of sacrifice (Hebrews). The event remains the same, and in reality all these interpretations are derived from the event itself. The unity of the Bible is to be found in God and in his redemptive activity which is the same from beginning to end. This great volume which has come to us from different times and circumstances, and which was produced and compiled over a span of some fifteen hundred years, nevertheless has just this one message that God is the Creator, Judge, Redeemer and Lord of all humanity.

## THEIR CHARACTERISTICS

The seven events which have been selected as the great events of the biblical record—the Fall, the Flood, Abraham, Exodus, Exile, Christ, Parousia—exhibit the same essential characteristics. They are all concerned with the relationship between God and humanity.

Each of these events is fundamental for the epoch between it and the next event. As the meaning of the event unfolds in the period which it opens, prophets and apostles supply the interpretation. They proclaim God's act of redemption and exhort the people to believe in and live by his grace. The whole New Testament is an interpretation of the event of Christ. The letters of Paul, the Letter to the Hebrews, Revelation, etc., are just as much a part of the event as the gospel record of the ministry, death, and Resurrection of Jesus. The event of Christ is not something that happened and was finished nineteen hundred years ago, it is a present reality. The whole epoch of the church down to the present time is determined and dominated by the event of Christ.

It has already been stated that each of these events embodies judgment, redemption, and promise. It is, of course, possible to say that of these three factors redemption is the central, essential, and primary consideration. God's constant and ultimate purpose is to redeem mankind. His conflict with the evil powers has this end in view. Judgment and promise could be regarded as subordinate elements in this great purpose of God. The Bible, however, speaks realistically and seriously of judgment as well as of redemption: of God's wrath as well as of his grace. God's work, which he has also given to the Son to perform, is to confer life and to execute judgment (John 5:21-22). Since Jesus speaks of the "cursed" who are to depart "into the eternal fire" (Matt. 25:41), it would seem that judgment, too, is an end in itself and represents a final act of God by which man is separated from him. If there are powers at work in the world which are hostile to God and opposed to his will, and if man himself participates in this opposition, the redemptive purpose of God must inevitably appear also as judgment.

The promise is also an essential factor in each event. The promise grows out of the event itself, or is deduced from it. The call of Abraham would have had no meaning without the promise of a new nation to be occupied. The redemption of the slaves out of Egypt would have had no meaning if there had been no land toward which they were to journey. The faith in Jesus as Christ and

Lord inevitably must be accompanied by a conviction that he will return and establish his kingdom.

Since the events stand in a continuous series, each event fulfills the promise of the previous event. The prophets of the Exile saw the return as the fulfillment of the promise to the patriarchs and to Israel. The disciples of Jesus saw in him the fulfillment of Scripture and of the Old Testament promises. Those who participated in the events of the Exodus, the return from Exile, and the coming of Christ expected each to be the final event, in which the purpose of God was about to be realized. It is only as an event passes and the course of the world continues that the promise of a new event becomes clear. Thus, at first the disciples did not expect two comings of Christ, and the triumphant return of Christ was considered a part of the one event they had witnessed. As the Parousia was delayed, the church began to look for a new event, a second coming, which would then be final. The next event is seen as a promise inherent in the previous event. When God made "this Jesus" whom they crucified "both Christ and Lord" and gave him "a name that is above every name," the promise of his presence and his return became a necessary part of the Christian message. Yet the promise is then no longer general and obscure, it is the promise of the return of him who "was put to death for our trespasses and raised for our justification" (Rom. 4:25).

Each event is an act of God. It is his coming and activity that produces the event. Both judgment and redemption are his personal acts and the result of his will. He sent the Flood, but he also provided the means of salvation for Noah and his house. He destroyed the pursuing Egyptian army, while he opened the way for Israel to proceed. The cloud and the pillar of fire were the symbols of his presence. The Exile was his judgment on Israel. "Who gave up Jacob to the spoiler, and Israel to the robbers? Was it not the Lord, against whom we have sinned?" (Isa. 42:24). But he is also the Redeemer. "I, I am He who blots out your transgressions for my own sake, and I will not remember your sins" (Isa. 43:25. Cf. Deut. 7:6-8). It was God who anointed Cyrus to be the deliverer of the exiles. At every point it is God who takes the initiative and makes the event come to pass.

These events occur in human history, and they are truly human events in which such men as Abraham, Moses, Cyrus, and Nehemiah are actors. These men were not automatons without any wills of their own. Moses can even argue with God and tell him that it is both dangerous and useless to go back to Egypt. Israel frequently rebelled against the covenant and went its own way. Nevertheless, it is God who acts in these events with sovereign power and right-

eousness, and at every point it is his will that must prevail. It is human history under God. Since it is God who acts, and since he acts with the final end always in view, the whole course of events is eschatalogical. Man stands before God at every point, not only on the last day.

Each event fulfills, completes, expands, and to a certain extent supplants the previous event. This may be expressed graphically. It might also be said that each event is a preparation for the next. The eschatological "fullness of time" is a part of each of these events. Each action occurs in accordance with "the definite plan and foreknowledge of God" (Acts 2:23). The events occur in an expanding series. The result is a progressive revelation of God's purpose. The general promise of the defeat of the serpent given to Adam and Eve becomes more definite in the call of Abraham and emerges more clearly still in the person of the Suffering Servant. The promise given to Adam, Noah, and Abraham hardly goes beyond the idea of possessing the earth, but in the prophecies of Isaiah and Jeremiah the promise is for a new type of people and a new order of righteousness and salvation for all peoples. When finally he who is the real Suffering Servant comes, his command is to "go and make disciples of all nations" (Matt. 28:19). Each event is new, a new turn in history which creates a new situation for men. The past is taken up, fulfilled, and expanded in each succeeding event.

This series of events, therefore, presents both continuity and discontinuity, both stability and progress. The events are not breaks with the past, nor points from which development goes on in a different direction. The miracle of changing the water into wine (John 2:1-11) undoubtedly means that the "new wine" of the gospel replaces the old ceremonial water of Judaism, but Jesus nevertheless used that water to produce the new. If God really has a purpose and a goal, and the Bible affirms that he has, there must be an organic unity and continuity in the development. Bishop Newbigin states: "[God's] tactics must vary but his fundamental strategy is the same. He may lay himself open to charges of incon-

sistency and infidelity to his promises, but a deeper understanding
of his promises will show that all that he has done has sprung from
one unchanging purpose—to have mercy upon all."[3] God's holy
and righteous will is always the same. The past is not repudiated,
but incorporated into the new order and thereby transformed. The
call of Abraham does not repudiate the covenant with Noah, nor
does the Exile nullify the Exodus. Each event is the fulfillment of
the promise already present in the preceding one.

It is, therefore, misleading to interpret the New Testament as
the new age which came in Christ when it is implied thereby that
the Old Testament was the old age under law, sin, and death, and
the New Testament the new age of grace, salvation, and life. It is
true that the New Testament emphasizes very strongly that a new
epoch has come now in the event of Christ: "The law was given
through Moses; grace and truth came through Jesus Christ" (John
1:17). "New wine is for fresh skins" (Mark 2:22). The gospel
of Christ is "the mystery hidden for ages and generations but now
made manifest to his saints" (Col. 1:26). "The prophets . . .
searched and inquired about this salvation" (I Peter 1:10). "The
mystery of Christ, which was not made known to the sons of men
in other generations as it has now been revealed to his holy apostles and prophets by the Spirit" (Eph. 3:4-5). Emphasis on a new
act and a new revelation is found, however, in connection with the
other events also. There are several such references in Isaiah: "Behold the former things have come to pass, and new things I now
declare; before they spring forth I tell you of them" (Isa. 42:9).
"Behold, I am doing a new thing; now it springs forth, do you not
perceive it?" (43:19). Compare Isa. 48:6, 65:17, 66:22; Jer.
31:22. The Exodus was also "a new thing," beginning a new era
in the history of God's dealings with men, as was the Flood and
the call of Abraham. At the end of the whole process God declares:
"Behold, I make all things new" (Rev. 21:5). It is natural that
those who stand close to the events as they happen, as Isaiah, Jere-

---

[3] J. E. L. Newbigin, *The Household of God* (New York, 1954), p. 46.

miah and the New Testament writers did, arrive at the conclusion that the event in which they participate far surpasses anything that has gone before. To them it is the eschatological hour of God's final triumph. This idea is not entirely mistaken, for each event fulfills and expands the previous events. The coming of Christ as the incarnate Son of God far surpassed anything that had happened so far. It will be surpassed only by the next event, the Parousia.

It is really unfortunate, therefore, that the Bible has been divided into the Old and the New Testaments as if there were two separate revelations. There is only one Bible, one revelation, one Word of God, which records the acts of God from the beginning to the final consummation. The coming of Christ was not a break with the past but its fulfillment, and it did not inaugurate an entirely new age. "Think not that I have come to abolish the law and the prophets; I have come not to abolish them but to fulfil them" (Matt. 5:17).

We are not justified, therefore, in dividing the biblical record into an old age and a new age. The Old Testament is also a record of God's redemptive activity, and men were saved by grace through faith in the Old Testament as well as in the New. The old age and the new age run parallel from the beginning to the end. The old age of law, sin, and death began when man fell into sin, and the new age of grace and life began when God came to fallen man with grace, mercy, and forgiveness. The Old Testament events were real acts of redemption, and the people then living were also God's redeemed people. God has been engaged in the activities of redemption and salvation from the beginning, and he "is working still." Whenever God comes to call and redeem his people, he brings them into the new age and into communion and fellowship with himself. When Paul wanted to use an example of one who was justified by faith, he went back to Abraham. The new age came in Christ, but it came also in God's visit to Adam and Eve, in the saving of Noah, in the call of Abraham, in the Exodus and in the return from the Exile. It will come also with the return of Christ when the eternal kingdom of God will be established. The

New Testament is not a book that is closed and finished. God's final purpose has not been accomplished as yet. The event of Christ inaugurated the age of preaching of the gospel in all the world, but this preaching clearly looks forward to a new event. "And this gospel of the kingdom will be preached throughout the whole world, as a testimony to all nations; and then the end will come" (Matt. 24:14).

## THEIR UNIVERSALITY

We have spoken as though the biblical record deals with God's relationship to all humanity, but actually we see that it deals with certain individuals and with a select people, whether Israel or the church. Throughout the Bible there is a tension between creation and election, between universalism and particularism. God is the Creator of all men, and he maintains all of life, but it would seem that at times he works with only a part of humanity, abandoning the rest to their own ways. It could be argued that the idea of universalism appears late in the biblical narrative. When the mission to the Gentiles begins and the missionaries go into all the world "to make disciples of all nations," the gospel becomes universal. Then all distinctions are taken away. "There is neither Jew nor Greek, there is neither slave nor free, there is neither male nor female; for you are all one in Christ Jesus" (Gal. 3:28).

The tension between creation and election has led scholars to differing interpretations of the biblical perspective. Arthur G. Hebert has outlined the biblical events as follows. (1) The Bible begins with a preface, chapters 1–11 of Genesis, which tells about the creation, the Fall, man's growing corruption, the Flood, and the dispersion of the people. This is the setting of the story. In this fallen, sinful world the action of God's redemptive activity takes place. (2) Chapters 12–50, which trace the patriarchs as individuals, serve as an introduction to the subsequent development. (3) The main story, from Exodus to the end of the Old Testament, contains the story of the founding of God's people and the history of God's dealings with them. It becomes increasingly clear as we follow the narrative, however, that this is not the final stage. A new event has to come: (4) the coming of Christ, with the founding of God's people, the church.[4]

Hebert's outline presents a great perspective of the biblical narrative, but it does not take all the factors into consideration. In making Israel and the church the main story, Hebert obscures the fact that God is concerned with all humanity. In this outline the church becomes the final goal of God's activity. Yet the Bible begins with humanity facing God and it ends with all humanity gathered before him. Israel and the church are not ends in themselves, they are the servants of God at a particular time to proclaim to all humanity the gospel of redemption. Another book by Hebert bears the significant subtitle, "A Study of the Fulfilment of the Old Testament in Jesus Christ and His Church."[5] When creation and the early mythical history are reduced to a preface, the church seems the only goal of the story and the universal aspect of the biblical narrative is obscured.

Gustaf Wingren, who discusses this exposition by Hebert, proposes a different outline. In his scheme chapters 1-11 of Genesis represent universal history. Here God is dealing with humanity as a whole. The relationship is precarious, however, and ends indecisively with the Tower of Babel and the dispersion of the people. At this point the universal history breaks off and God begins to deal with a special people, Abraham and his descendants. The rest of humanity, the nations, are ignored except insofar as they touch on Israel's history, although there are indications that this is a temporary arrangement. In time God fulfills his promise in the coming of Christ. In Christ the story returns to the universal line. When the universality of the gospel has been fully apprehended by the church and the mission to the Gentiles is thoroughly begun, Paul can relate his message to the promise to Abraham: "By you all the families of the earth will bless themselves." Now the purpose of God has become clear, and the gospel is to be proclaimed

---

[4]Arthur G. Hebert, *Scripture and the Faith* (London, 1947), pp. 23 ff.
[5]Hebert, *The Throne of David* (London, 1941).

to all the peoples in all the world.[6] This outline can be represented graphically.

To us, however, it seems unnecessary to differentiate between the history of Israel and universal history. The tension between creation and election, between the universal and the particular, is characteristic of the whole Bible. The elect always stand over against the whole of humanity. Abel was accepted, Cain was not. Some antediluvian patriarchs like Enoch "walked with God," while the mass of humanity became corrupt and degenerate. Noah was saved, but other antediluvians perished. The contrast continues: Abraham and the Chaldeans, Israel and the Egyptians, Israel and the nations, the Remnant and the apostate people, the "little flock" and the Jews, the church and the world. In every age God has an elect people and elect individuals who stand in a special relationship to him. There is no more justification for regarding the history of Israel as a special dispensation than for regarding the whole Bible as recording God's dealings with selected individuals and peoples—such as Noah, Abraham, Israel and the church—to the exclusion of others. So to regard the Bible would be to misinterpret it and to deny its universal perspective. God is the God of all humanity, and his activity in the Bible has reference to all humanity, even when the story deals primarily with one people like Israel.

Both the individuals and the peoples whom God elects are chosen to serve his universal redemptive purpose. If God were to elect some for their own sake without reference to humanity as a whole, his government of the world would seem to be capricious and arbitrary. On the contrary, the New Testament insists that "God shows no partiality. In every nation any one who fears him and does what is right is acceptable to him" (Acts 10:34-35). Since it is God who makes the choice, the elect become a part of his eternal and universal purpose. "An election that was merely favouritism would have little in common with universalism, but an election that is conceived in terms of purpose is entirely consistent with universalism."[7] The elect are to be the instruments of God in carrying out his purpose for humanity. Election is for service.

The conviction that the elect are to serve the Lord in reference to "the nations" is expressed rather frequently even in the Old Testament. A very significant passage is recorded in two of the eighth century prophets:

> It shall come to pass in the latter days
>    that the mountain of the house of the Lord
> shall be established as the highest of the mountains,
>    and shall be raised above the hills;
> and all the nations shall flow to it,
>    and many peoples shall come, and say:
> "Come, let us go up to the mountain of the Lord,
>    to the house of the God of Jacob;
> that he may teach us his ways
>    and that we may walk in his paths."
> For out of Zion shall go forth the law,
>    and the word of the Lord from Jerusalem.
>                     —Isa. 2:2-3; Mic. 4:1-2

Paul justifies the mission to the Gentiles by citing Isa. 52:15: "They shall see who have never been told of him, and they shall understand who have never heard of him" (Rom. 15:21). In the same chapter he quotes Ps. 18:49, Ps. 117:1, Deut. 32:43, and Isa. 11:10, in order to prove that God intended the Gentiles to re-

---

[7]Harold H. Rowley, *The Biblical Doctrine of Election* (London, 1950), p. 63.

ceive the gospel. Paul of course applies these passages to the present, but it is nevertheless significant that he can find applicable passages in the Old Testament. These Old Testament writers were talking about Israel's mission, not about Paul's. Other passages he might have quoted would have been just as pertinent. When the Ark had been brought up to Jerusalem, David appointed "that thanksgiving be sung to the Lord by Asaph and his brethren."

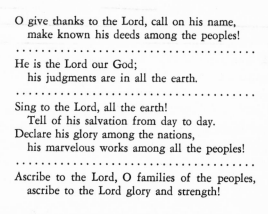

> O give thanks to the Lord, call on his name,
>     make known his deeds among the peoples!
> . . . . . . . . . . . . . . . . . . . . . . . . . . . . . . . . . . .
> He is the Lord our God;
>     his judgments are in all the earth.
> . . . . . . . . . . . . . . . . . . . . . . . . . . . . . . . . . . .
> Sing to the Lord, all the earth!
>     Tell of his salvation from day to day.
> Declare his glory among the nations,
>     his marvelous works among all the peoples!
> . . . . . . . . . . . . . . . . . . . . . . . . . . . . . . . . . . .
> Ascribe to the Lord, O families of the peoples,
>     ascribe to the Lord glory and strength!

This thanksgiving is recorded in I Chron. 16:8-36, and it is found also in Psalm 96, Ps. 105:1-15, and Ps. 106:1, 47, 48. All these passages have been applied exclusively to the New Testament as if they had no meaning for the contemporary situation, even though they clearly express the consciousness of Israel's mission to the world. Even in the call of the prophet Jeremiah, God declares to him: "Before I formed you in the womb I knew you, and before you were born I consecrated you; I appointed you a prophet to the nations" (Jer. 1:5). The last of the prophetic books of the Old Testament contains this striking passage:

> From the rising of the sun to its setting my name is great among the nations, and in every place incense is offered to my name, and a pure offering; for my name is great among the nations, says the Lord of hosts.
>
> —Mal. 1:11

It may be freely admitted that the ideas of universality and service are more clearly and frequently expressed in the New Testament. The recognition of the universality of the gospel came to the fore finally in the mission to the Gentiles, but this did not take place without a struggle against those who regarded the messianic salvation as a special privilege of the Jewish people and insisted that the Gentiles must first of all become Jews. There is, however, in the whole Bible a progressively clearer recognition that God is the God of all peoples and that he is concerned with humanity as a whole. Those whom he elects have an obligation, therefore, to make his wonderful works known among the children of men. When monotheism became firmly established in Israel, and it was recognized that God was the Creator of all men, the concern for "the nations" could not be entirely avoided. The biblical doctrine of creation stands guard against any attempt to make one people or a selected few the exclusive object of God's concern. The election involved an obligation to keep and preserve the revelation of God, to glorify his name, and to proclaim "the Word of the Lord" to all nations.

The election to service is clearly expressed also in the great biblical events. Adam and Eve are to become the progenitors of one through whom the curse on the earth will be lifted (cf. Rom. 8: 20 ff.) and redemption will come to all the world. Noah was saved not for his own sake alone but in order that his family should replenish the earth. Abraham received a blessing so great that all the nations of the earth were to covet it for themselves. Israel was to be "a light to the nations, that my salvation may reach to the end of the earth" (Isa. 49:6). Jesus selected the twelve "to be with him, and to be sent out to preach" (Mark 3:14).

Election, therefore, is closely associated with these redemptive events. God deals here with elect individuals and peoples, but because it is God who deals with them, they become involved in his eternal and universal purpose. This is the way Paul interprets his own experience: "But when he who had set me apart before I was born, and had called me through his grace, was pleased to reveal

his Son to me, *in order that* I might preach him among the Gentiles . . ." (Gal. 1:15-16) (italics added). Through these redemptive events God selects his people for the service he expects them to
perform. Although the event may concern only a few people directly, it is nevertheless a part of God's whole plan for humanity.

Certain factors must be taken into account, however, when we
speak of election to service. When we try to interpret God's eternal purpose and trace the steps whereby he carries it forward, we
are dealing with a subject that—even with the revelation given us
in the Bible—we can fathom only in part. It is ever true that "my
ways are not your ways, and my thoughts are not your thoughts."
In general it is quite plain that God selects his own to be his witnesses, but there are certain factors which complicate both the
choice and the service.

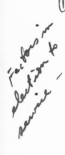

In the first place, God selects those who are able and willing to
serve his purpose. Noah, Abraham, the Israelites, and the apostles
were chosen because they possessed qualities that enabled them to
become bearers of the revelation and instruments of his purpose.
These qualities are not to be judged by human standards. Over
and over again it is emphasized that God did not choose Israel as a
great, numerous, or powerful people (Deut. 7:6 ff.; 9:5 ff.). Paul
says: "God chose what is foolish in the world to shame the wise,
God chose what is weak in the world to shame the strong, God
chose what is low and despised in the world, even things that are
not, to bring to nothing things that are, so that no human being
might boast in the presence of God" (I Cor. 1:27-29). God himself is the sole judge of the qualifications.

In the second place, the elect do not always recognize and acknowledge the obligation to service which election imposes upon
them. They sometimes act like Jonah, who was disgruntled and
angry because God wanted a Gentile city like Nineveh to hear the
word. "It is probable that in [the thought of the author of the
Book of Jonah] Jonah stood for the nation, and his mission to
Nineveh for Israel's mission to the world,"[8] but Jonah and Israel

[8]*Ibid.*, p. 67.

were unwilling to carry out that mission. It was one thing for the prophet to see that Israel's mission was to be a witness until "the earth shall be full of the knowledge of the Lord as the waters cover the sea" (Isa. 11:9), but it was quite another thing for Israel to decide how far she was willing to carry out that program. The church has received her great commission to "go into all the world and make disciples of all the nations," but she has often lost sight of the purpose for which she was chosen. The elect may refuse the call to service. Whether after such a refusal they still remain the elect, or the election passes to someone else, to a remnant, is another question.

In the third place, since God is the Creator of all men and deals  with all humanity, he may select even the unwilling and the recalcitrant to do his will and further his purpose. Of Pharaoh in Egypt, the Bible even says that God "hardened his heart and the heart of his servants" (Exod. 10:1) in order that the divine purpose might be fulfilled: "For this purpose have I let you live, to show you my power, so that my name may be declared throughout all the earth" (Exod. 9:16). Just as Israel carried out God's judgments on the Canaanites, so the Egyptians, Assyrians, Babylonians, and other nations carried out his judgments on Israel. As God selects men to carry out his redemptive purposes, so does he select them to carry out his judgments. In the New Testament, Judas, Pilate, and the Jewish authorities make their own decisions, but at the same time they serve "the eternal counsel and foreknowledge of God." Since God rules in the life and affairs of all men, all may be used in one way or another in his service. But election proper means being accepted into the fellowship with God and serving him in willing obedience and in understanding of his purpose.

In the fourth place, what God does in these events as he selects those who are to serve him is indicative of what he does for all humanity. God is the universal savior. That he has chosen Israel, redeemed her, and made her his own does not mean that he has abandoned the rest of mankind to inevitable and total destruction. In the biblical events God makes known his will that "all men [are] to be saved and to come to the knowledge of the truth" (I Tim. 2:4). That he loves Israel does not mean that he loves no one else. "God so loved the *world.*" It became clear to Peter that "God shows no partiality, but in every nation any one who fears him and does what is right is acceptable to him." Compare Jonah 4:11: "Should I not pity Nineveh, that great city, in which there are more than a hundred and twenty thousand persons who do not know their right hand from their left, and also much cattle?" Peter also says: "In past generations he allowed all the nations to walk in their own ways; yet he did not leave himself without witness, for he did good and gave you from heaven rains and fruitful seasons, satisfying your hearts with food and gladness" (Acts 14:16-17).

In his relationship with humanity, God has always dealt with individuals and with particular groups of people. Even today it is primarily through the church that God makes himself known as Creator and Redeemer. Nonetheless, the Bible expressly warns the elect against the folly of believing that they are his favorites in their own right, or that he is concerned with them alone:

> "Are you not like the Ethiopians to me,
>   O people of Israel?" says the Lord.
> "Did I not bring up Israel from the land of Egypt,
>   and the Philistines from Caphtor and the Syrians from Kir?"
>
> —*Amos 9:7*

His infinite love has ways of manifesting itself even to men outside the biblical tradition. Wherever men lift their hearts and hands in supplication to a power above on whom they depend, we have a right to believe that the God and Father of our Lord Jesus Christ, the God of all grace, has called them also and has received them into his fellowship. The biblical record and the events are universal also in the sense that the gracious, redemptive activity of God revealed here embraces all his creatures in the vast expanse of his mercy and grace.

MAN'S UNDERSTANDING OF HIMSELF IN THESE EVENTS

At this point we must distinguish between the eternal purpose of God expressed in the biblical events and the human understanding and interpretation of them. Man sees in part and understands in part. His conception of each event is therefore limited, and must be revised as time goes on and further revelation is given. If there is in the Bible a concept of progressive revelation, then man's understanding of the events should change and become clearer.

Despite progress toward understanding, man's situation is essentially the same in every period. Each man stands between the event of the past and a future event contained in the promise. What God has done in the past constitutes the basis of his faith. He looks back to an act of God as an act of redemption, which is not simply an act of the past but a present reality. He is convinced that what God has done in the past is what God is doing for him now in the present, and will do also in the future. Thus he looks forward to the promised new event which will mark the completion of God's purpose and the consummation of His plans. Faith rests on God's work in the past and on man's experience of the reality of God's redemptive work in the present, and hope is directed toward the promise of a new event to come.

If we could ask a man who lived during the Israelite monarchy, for instance, what made him certain that he and his people were the people of God, he would point back to the call of Abraham and the Exodus. In these events God had demonstrated his choice and redemption of Israel, and these events were the primary objects of his faith. They constituted the basis of the covenant relationship which made God his God and his people God's people. He might mention a host of other events in which God demonstrated his care for the Israelites and his concern for their welfare, but Abraham and the Exodus would remain the basic facts. The psalmists celebrated these events and the prophets used them in order to call the people back to repentance and obedience. The recurrent celebration of the Passover, when the ancient story was rehearsed and the ceremonials explained, served to perpetuate and strengthen the conviction that God had then chosen Israel and made them his people. Psalm 136 gave an account of what God had done in creation, in the Exodus, and in Israel's history, and the response of the people was repeated over and over again: "For his steadfast love endures forever." The prophet of the Exile exhorted his people:

> Hearken to me, you who pursue deliverance,
>     you who seek the Lord;
> look to the rock from which you were hewn,
>     and to the quarry from which you were digged.
> Look to Abraham your father
>     and to Sarah who bore you;
> for when he was but one I called him,
>     and I blessed him and made him many.
>
> —*Isa. 51:1-2*

It was not Abraham as a person but God's redemptive act and his choice which constituted the foundation of the faith of the prophet and his confidence that God was still Israel's God. God's steadfast love and faithfulness which had been revealed in these past acts were the foundation of the Israelites' confidence that God would redeem them out of all their troubles.

In these events there was also a promise for the future. The man living in the time of the judges, before Canaan was wholly occupied, could have said with Paul: "I am sure that he who began a good work in [us] will bring it to completion" (Phil. 1:6). To the people who experienced the redemption out of Egypt the promise referred quite realistically to the earthly land of Canaan. As time went on and the land proved to be less than they had expected, the promise was transformed into a promise of a new kind of person and a more intimate relationship to God. The promise, though, was an integral part of the event of redemption. The people lived in a tension between what they were now as the people of God and what they would become when God should finish the work already begun.

Man stands in this situation in every age. We who are living today look back to the events of the past, especially to the event of Christ. The death and resurrection of Christ is for us *the* event through which we have been redeemed and become the children of God. It means that he is the living Lord who now comes to men with redemption and life, but it is meaningless unless we are persuaded with Paul that God will finish what he has begun. The Christian, too, stands between an event in the past and a promised event which is the object of his hope. Just as he is convinced that he is saved by grace through faith in Jesus Christ, so is he certain that this salvation will be completed in the future when God establishes his eternal kingdom. Faith and hope are thus the constituents in man's experience of salvation. The object of faith is God's acts in the past and the present, and the object of hope is the promise. If this promise of a consummation had no reality, the event of the Cross and the Resurrection would also become meaningless.

In this sense, there is no essential difference between the situation of the people in the Old Testament and our situation. They walked in faith based on an event of redemption and revelation, and they were journeying toward a goal set before them by God's promise. They lived by faith in God and were saved by his grace. The object of their faith was the living God who had revealed himself in mighty acts and was now the faithful God of the covenant. We have a longer history of God's revelation of himself and of his redemptive activity. God's character and purpose have been revealed to us in Christ. We are the heirs of all that the fathers have experienced and learned of the wonderful works of God with the children of men. Essentially our situation is the same. We, too, walk by faith in God as Abraham and the saints of old did, and we look for the fulfillment of the promise that was given to the fathers as well as to us.

The people who lived during or after each of these events always regarded the latest one as the greatest of them. The Exodus was greater and more comprehensive than the call of Abraham. In the prophecies of Isaiah and Jeremiah the return from the Exile was greater than anything that had gone before. Now the Lord "will make a new covenant with the house of Israel and the house of Judah, not like the covenant which I made with their fathers when I took them by the hand to bring them out of the land of Egypt, my covenant which they broke, though I was their husband, says the Lord. But this is the covenant which I will make with the house of Israel after those days, says the Lord: I will put my law within them, and I will write it upon their hearts; and I will be their God, and they shall be my people" (Jer. 31:31-33). The prophet was not referring to the new covenant of the New Testament, but to the covenant which God would make now with the returning exiles. To the people of the New Testament the event of Christ was so great and mighty a work of God that everything in the past was dwarfed by comparison. This was God's real act of redemption. What had gone before was preparatory, fragmentary and inconclusive. God had spoken of old to the fathers by the prophets in various ways, "but in these last days he has spoken to us by a Son" (Heb. 1:1-2). This conception is not only inevitable but also correct. Since there is a progression in these events, the latest event is greater than the preceding ones, but it must not be interpreted as a break with the past, or a repudiation of the others. It is greater because it completes and fulfills the past. So also the New Testament pictures the next event, the Parousia, as the greatest of all because it fulfills all the past in a final consummation.

In the human expectation the next event, or the event just happening, is always regarded as the last. To Noah the sign of the rainbow meant that there was to be no more destruction. Abraham expected to settle at once in Canaan, where his descendants would be a great people and would walk forever in the ways of the Lord. The people of the Exodus were going to a land flowing with milk and honey where they would abide forever. The prophets of the Exile expected the new age to dawn as soon as they returned to Jerusalem. The later messianic expectation of the Jews centered on a Messiah whose coming would establish the kingdom, a hope they held in any of several forms. The messianic kingdom was sometimes thought of as temporary, lasting four hundred or a thousand years, after which the end would come. Most frequently, however, it was expected to be everlasting. They did not expect two comings of the Messiah. The next event would be the last and would usher in the new age.

These expectations were not fulfilled. The people who invaded Canaan found it a difficult country. Not only did native inhabitants have to be subdued and absorbed; surrounding enemies were forever harassing the newcomers. When the kingdom was finally established in the reign of David and Solomon, internal dissension began and the kingdom was divided into the two mutually hostile parts, Israel and Judah. It became increasingly clear that the land of Canaan was not the fulfillment of the promise to Abraham. Neither did the vision of the prophet of the Exile materialize. The new nation that arose was conceived in isolationism and dedicated to the proposition that its people had an exclusive relationship to God.

In the New Testament the death, resurrection, ascension, and return of Christ are conceived of as one event. The disciples believed him to be the Messiah who was to establish the kingdom. When Jesus began to foretell his own suffering and death, they were horrified and Peter "rebuked" him for talking in that fashion (Mark 8:31-33). They expected him to be the King Messiah who would give two of them the privilege of sitting one on his right side and one on his left in his glory (Mark 10:35 ff.). Even after the resurrection they asked him: "Lord, will you at this time restore the kingdom to Israel?" (Acts 1:6). The early sermons in Acts declare that God has made this crucified Jesus both Christ and Lord, "whom heaven must receive until the time for establishing all that God spoke by the mouth of his holy prophets from of old" (Acts 3:21). Paul himself indicates that he expected the return of Christ to take place during his own lifetime (I Thess. 4:15). The delay of the Parousia had the result that the expected coming of the Messiah grew into two comings. He had already come, he had gone back to heaven, and he was to return again. The second coming then was going to be the last event.

Just as the Jewish expectation was waiting for a final event, so the church waits for the return of Christ, which will mark the end of history and the final consummation. It might of course be argued that, since this expectation has so often met with disappointment, we really ought not to expect any final event at all. Maybe there is a long series of events still awaiting humanity! In view of the use of atomic power for destruction, maybe a cataclysmic event ahead will destroy the world as we know it and cause a new start for mankind. The possibilities are infinite. We may as well admit that God has not given us a road map or a blueprint of the future. We have his revelation of his will and purpose in the redemptive acts recorded in the Bible. These past events we can know and analyze. They tell us the character and purpose of God. This record is the foundation of our faith. God has also given us a promise that he will surely finish his work of redemption in his own time and in his own way. When and how this will be, we do not know. In the meantime we stand like the Old Testament saints between the event of the past and the promise, and we walk in faith toward the goal set before us. We are left finally with faith in God, this God who has revealed himself in the biblical events as Creator, Redeemer, and Lord.

## THE EVENTS AS REVELATION

These biblical events constitute the core of God's revelation of himself to men. Here God reveals himself as Judge and Redeemer. In the Exodus God stretched forth his strong arm and led the people out of slavery into the promised land. In this experience of redemption they learned to know God as their God. He repeated this work in bringing the exiles back through the wilderness to their native land. The New Testament declares that "God was in Christ reconciling the world to himself." When God by his grace redeems man out of his bondage of sin and death, then man learns to know God.

This activity of God in judgment and redemption, therefore, is revelation. The word revelation should not suggest drawing aside a curtain or unveiling a picture to see a finished object previously hidden from us. Revelation in the Bible involves God's creative action. It is given in the way he deals with men. We learn to know a person by his actions. We cannot know a corpse, which neither acts nor expresses itself. It is by men's words and actions that we learn to know their character and being. In the same way God reveals his character and purpose in the way he acts. Not only "God speaks and reveals himself," but "God acts and reveals himself."

God reveals himself in his work. Just as God's "invisible nature, namely, his eternal power and deity, has been clearly perceived in the things that have been made" (Rom. 1:20), so his eternal purpose for mankind can be seen most clearly in these acts of his in human history. "The Old Testament religion did not take shape through mythological and metaphysical speculations, but through the prophetic encounters with Yahweh."[9] These "prophetic encounters" were the biblical events in which the prophets saw the activity of God and interpreted it for the people. Both the prophets and the psalmists reminded the people that God had made them his people through his redemptive activity in these events, and that they were bound to live as his people in faith and obedience. Their faith in God and their knowledge of God were anchored in the events of their history.

To say that these biblical events are acts of God, and that they reveal the character and purpose of God, is a confession of faith. There is no way of proving that the call of Abraham was really a call of God. His experience was similiar to that of thousands of young men who have heard and obeyed such an injunction as "Go out from your fatherland," or "Go west, young man." The escape of a group of slaves from Egypt would be a very minor event in any secular history. The escape from the Red Sea was not even

---

[9] Gösta Lindeskog, "The Theology of Creation in the Old and the New Testaments," in *The Root of the Vine* (London, 1953), p. 5.

miraculous in the popular sense of that word. An east wind blew and drove the water back (Exod. 14:21). But the prophetic spirits of Israel saw the hand of the Lord in all these episodes. It was not Moses but God who redeemed them from Egypt and brought them to the promised land. There is no way of proving that Paul was right when he said "God was in Christ reconciling the world to himself," but millions of people in the history of the church have found in these words a reality which has given meaning to their lives.

The people of the Bible confess their faith in God by telling what God has done. They do not try to define God in conceptual and philosophic terms; rather, they point to God's acts in their own history. When children asked formally, as part of the Passover observance, what these ceremonies meant, they were told the ancient story of the marvelous act of God in Egypt (Deut. 6:20-24). In Psalm 136 the psalmist expresses his faith by reciting the story of Israel, and the people answer with the refrain, "His steadfast love endures forever." Even the New Testament confession of Christ is made in terms of what Christ has done: "He was manifested in the flesh, vindicated in the Spirit, seen by angels, preached among the nations, believed on in the world, taken up in glory" (I Tim. 3:16). Even the great christological passage in Phil. 2:5-11 is a straightforward account of One who "was in the form of God," became man, humbled himself, became obedient unto death, and was exalted to the right hand of God and given a name that is above every name. There is nothing here of speculation as to the nature of Christ, but only a restatement of the incarnation, death, resurrection, and exaltation of Jesus.

In a similar way the church's confession in the words of the Apostles' Creed is a confession of God in his work. In this confession we acknowledge God as Creator, Redeemer, and Sanctifier. Luther explains the three articles of the creed: As Creator, God has "given and still preserves to me my body and soul" and "provides abundantly for all the needs of my life." As Redeemer, he who is true God and true man has "redeemed me, a lost and condemned creature, bought me and freed me from all sins, from death, and from the power of the devil . . . in order that I might be his own, live under him in his kingdom, and serve him." As Sanctifier, the Holy Spirit "calls, gathers, enlightens and sanctifies the whole Christian Church on earth, and preserves it in union with Christ in true faith; in which Christian Church he daily forgives abundantly all my sins, and the sins of all believers."

Both the Bible and the church confess their faith in God by giving an account of what God has done for man's life and salvation. Obviously, we can know God only as he has manifested himself in these mighty acts. We cannot know God as he is in himself, but only as he has revealed himself as our Creator, Redeemer, and Sanctifier.

The biblical record is a record "from faith to faith;" i.e., it is an expression of faith, and it is given in order to produce faith. The Bible is history under the aspect of eternity. The faith of the prophets, evangelists, and apostles tells us that this is God's work: God's dealings with men. Here God has made known his character and his purpose for man's salvation and life. Although this confession may be denied or rejected or dismissed as pure foolishness, as Paul was perfectly aware (I Cor. 1:18 ff.), the Bible is written from first to last in this faith. This is God's world. He has made it and he rules it. It has become a hostile, evil, fallen world, in rebellion against God and opposed to his will. But God has not abandoned it. He is at work in judgment and redemption, and his purpose is unwavering. He calls upon men to surrender their lives to him, to trust in him, and to wait patiently for the fulfillment of the promise. He has already shown his mighty power; he will reveal himself still more fully when the goal is reached and the kingdom is finally established.

# 3.

# Prophecy and Fulfillment

"Jesus came into Galilee, preaching the gospel of God, and saying, 'The time is fulfilled, and the kingdom of God is at hand; repent, and believe in the gospel'" (Mark 1:14-15). The fundamental faith of the New Testament Christians was that Jesus had come into the world to fulfill all that was spoken in the Scriptures and all the promises that God had made of old. If our interpretation of the biblical perspective as seen in the great events is correct, the expectation of the early Christians is understandable. As each event completes, fulfills, and expands the previous events, so the event of Christ is the culmination and realization of all that has gone before. He fulfills God's purpose in judgment and redemption. In the New Testament view, all the promises, from Adam to the Suffering Servant, found their fulfillment in him.

The early Christians took this view because they thought of Jesus' return as a part of the one event. Although he had indeed gone back to heaven, very shortly he would return on the clouds of heaven to establish his everlasting kingdom. God had made him both Messiah and Lord that through him everything the holy prophets had spoken of old might be accomplished. They could speak of him, therefore, as the Fulfiller of *all* the promises of God. Even when the second coming was postponed, the church could call him Fulfiller, for the One who is to return is the same crucified and risen Lord, "the Lamb that was slain and has redeemed us to God." Since he is the Lord, it is he who will reign. The delay of the Parousia has necessitated the concept of two comings, and the immediate unity of the first and the second comings expressed in the New Testament can no longer be maintained. The purpose of the first coming was the Cross and the Resurrection, and the purpose of the second coming is the consummation. All this has been promised in the Scriptures, and all will be fulfilled in and through this crucified and risen Lord.

The disciples confessed their faith in him as the Messiah during the ministry in Galilee, when Peter, speaking for all of them, declared: "You are the Christ [the Messiah], the Son of the living God" (Matt. 16:16). As they went up to Jerusalem, they evidently expected that he would openly claim messiahship, thus beginning the drama of the end. Their faith was severely shaken by the Crucifixion. The two disciples on the way to Emmaus told the stranger sorrowfully, "but we had hoped that he was the one to redeem Israel;" this they believed no more, until their encounter with the risen Lord changed their mood of defeat into a triumphant faith in him.

The event they now witnessed was something new. It was a new act of God, unexpected and marvelous. The Messiah turned out to be a strange figure such as the people had never expected. In order to understand, interpret, and proclaim this new event it was necessary to examine the old Scriptures anew and to see how God's plan had been prepared and executed. The new act of God had to be related to the Old Testament and understood in the whole perspective of God's previous dealings with Israel. Thus driven to a reexamination of the Old Testament, the early Christians came to the conclusion that this new event of Christ was the fulfillment of all that God had spoken. What had happened in Jerusalem was not an accident; it had come "according to the definite plan and foreknowledge of God." It had happened "according to the Scriptures."

The New Testament bears abundant witness to this faith of the early Christians that Jesus fulfills all Scripture. Jesus himself is reported to have emphasized this fact. When he appeared to the two disciples on the way to Emmaus, he chided them: "O foolish men and slow of heart to believe all that the prophets have spoken! Was it not necessary that the Christ should suffer these things and enter into his glory?" "And beginning with Moses and all the prophets, he interpreted to them in all the scriptures the things concerning himself" (Luke 24:25-27). The emphasis on *all* is obvious. A similar statement by Jesus occurs later in the same chapter. "These are my words which I spoke to you, while I was still with you, that everything written about me in the law of Moses and the prophets and the psalms must be fulfilled." "Then he opened their minds to understand the scriptures" (24:44-45). There are several similar statements by Jesus. "Let the scriptures be fulfilled" (Mark 14:49). "Everything that is written of the Son of man by the prophets will be accomplished" (Luke 18:31). "You search the scriptures . . . and it is they that bear witness to me" (John 5:39).

The early sermons in Acts all declare that Jesus has fulfilled the Scriptures. Peter, speaking to the people in Solomon's Portico, quoted Moses' statement about a future prophet, and then added: "And all the prophets who have spoken, from Samuel and those who came afterwards, also proclaimed these days" (Acts 3:24). Philip was asked to explain Isaiah 53 to the Ethiopian eunuch, and "beginning with this scripture he told him the good news of Jesus" (Acts 8:35). "What God promised" includes everything in his purpose which God had revealed in the Old Testament; and this had now been fulfilled in Christ (cf. Acts 13:32 ff.).

The earliest use of "according to the scriptures" in the New Testament comes from Paul. The confession he received states "that Christ died for our sins in accordance with the scriptures, that he was buried, that he was raised on the third day in accordance with the scriptures" (I Cor. 15:3-4). Paul writes that this confession is "of first importance," that he has received it and also transmitted it, that it is the common kerygma which all the preachers proclaim and the common faith. "Whether then it was I or they, so we preach and so you believed."

There is no conscious attempt in any of these passages to quote any particular Old Testament passage. It is simply asserted that Jesus fulfills all Scripture. There are very few attempts among early Christian writers to supply any particular "proof texts" in this connection. The Christian message did not consist in propositions that required proofs; it was a proclamation of events, acts of God, which had happened according to his eternal purpose. This proclamation testifies to the faith of the early church that in Jesus all the promises and the whole purpose of God were being fulfilled. The entire Old Testament—Moses, the prophets and the psalms— bears witness to Jesus as the Chosen One of God.

Their references to the Scriptures and to Moses, the prophets and the psalms indicate that the early Christians conceived of the entire Old Testament as a revelation of God's redemptive purpose. What they had witnessed in Christ was a new event, but it was not contrary to, or a departure from, this purpose. The events recorded in the Old Testament were similar in nature and characteristics to the event of Christ. What God had done now was "apart from law, although the law and the prophets bear witness to it"(Rom. 3:21). What Paul means here is not simply that certain prophecies in the Old Testament tell of the coming of Christ, but rather that the whole Old Testament witnesses and records the same redemptive activity of God which is now revealed in Christ. The Old Testament does not witness to "law righteousness" or "a righteousness of my own," but to a righteousness from God through faith. "Thus Abraham 'believed God, and it was reckoned to him as righteousness' " (Gal. 3:6). The redemptive activity of God which began as soon as man fell into sin now reached its decisive point in the death and resurrection of Jesus Christ.

It is difficult to see how the New Testament Christians could proclaim this fulfillment of Scripture unless they thought in quite general terms about the purpose of God for man's redemption. In fact, it is easier to understand how they could arrive at this conviction that Jesus fulfilled *all* Scripture than it is to find specific texts to prove this proposition in the Old Testament. When Paul said that "Christ died for our sins in accordance with the scriptures," was he thinking of Isaiah 53? Why then did he not quote it? Was he not thinking rather of the whole Old Testament tradition, and including all the events of God's redemptive activity and all the ideas of suffering and sacrifices that had been recorded? Where in all the Old Testament, with the exception of second Isaiah—which had never been interpreted messianically—had it been said that the Messiah was to suffer and die and on the third day rise again? Although very few specific passages could be quoted, the early Christians were convinced that what had happened in Christ was according to the *purpose* of God as revealed in the Scriptures.

Their faith was not based primarily on exact similarities between what had been said in the past and the events in the life of Jesus, but represented a conviction that God who had been at work in judgment and redemption in the past had now come in Christ to finish his work. It was their understanding of history as the events of God that led them to the conviction "God was in Christ reconciling the world to himself." The people of the early church were familiar with the Old Testament. They had a broad knowledge of God's redemptive acts and of his purpose. This steadfast purpose, they saw, had now been realized in Christ. They believed themselves to be the people "upon whom the end of the ages has come" (I Cor. 10:11): an end that was the fulfillment and realization of the redemptive activity and of the grand design of God's eternal purpose.

The faith of the early disciples was faith in Jesus as they had learned to know him in their association with him, and especially faith in him as the risen and living Lord. Their proclamation of this faith and their theology involved "an interpretation of history, a confessional recital of historical events as the acts of God, events which led backward to the beginning of history and forward to its end."[1] Their attitude toward the Old Testament writers was based primarily on the belief that God had directed the course of biblical events in the past, and that he was doing the same now in the events

---

[1] Wright, *op. cit.*, p. 57.

of Christ and the church. This was the faith and the interpretation
of the significance of Christ with which they started. The new
event realizes, fulfills, and expands all that has gone before. The
present can be understood only in the context of God's whole revelation and in the perspective of his deeds and promises recorded in
the Scriptures. Even the risen Lord did not simply tell them the
significance of his death and resurrection but rather "opened their
minds to understand the scriptures."

"THUS IT WAS FULFILLED"

Besides emphasizing the fulfillment of all Scripture, the New
Testament refers to a number of specific prophecies as fulfilled in
the life and ministry of Jesus. The references range from such obvious and significant events as the Triumphal Entry, which Jesus
himself may have arranged, to such obscure passages as "Out of
Egypt have I called my son" (Matt. 2:15) and "He shall be called
a Nazarene" (2:23). Some of them seem to have very little to do
with the mission of Jesus as the Savior of the world or with God's
redemptive purpose in history. These quotations are introduced by
a specific formula, "that what was spoken by the prophets might be
fulfilled," or "then was fulfilled what was spoken by the prophet."
    The presence of these formula quotations of fulfillment in the
Gospel narratives raises the question which was primary, the belief
that Jesus fulfilled all Scriptures, or the belief in the fulfillment of
certain specific prophecies. Did the early Christians start with a
faith in Jesus as the complete Fulfiller of God's eternal purpose
"according to the Scriptures," or did they, seeing in his life and
ministry details which fulfilled specific prophecies, conclude from
these instances that he was the Anointed of God and the Savior of
the world? If the latter were the case, the argument from the fulfillment of prophecy would loom very large as a foundation of their
faith. Did they start with individual prophecies and move toward
a general conception of fulfillment, or did they start with their
faith in him as Christ and Lord, and then on the basis of this faith
find individual instances of fulfillment? In the previous paragraphs

we have suggested that the New Testament bears witness to the
latter course. If this is true, we must search for an explanation of
how the argument from prophecy arose and became a part of the
New Testament record.

The experience of the disciples as recorded in the Gospels indicates that they came to believe in Jesus as the Messiah through their
own association with him. In the Synoptic Gospels we see how
Jesus called them and instructed them, and finally how they were
able through Peter to make the great confession, "You are the
Christ, the Son of the living God." There is no suggestion that they
came to this conviction on the basis of arguments from prophecy,
or by seeing Jesus do or say something that fulfilled a specific word
from the Old Testament. The formula quotations are comments
introduced by the evangelists; it is not suggested that these passages
occurred to the disciples at the time when the events took place.
The Gospel of John indicates that it was only later, after the Resurrection, that the fulfillment of Scripture occurred to them: "His
disciples did not understand this at first; but when Jesus was glori-
fied, then they remembered that this had been written of him and
had been done to him" (John 12:16; cf. 2:22). The disciples were
familiar with Scripture and with the expectations that clustered
around "the coming One." They joined him because they believed
they had found "him of whom Moses in the law and also the
prophets wrote," but they came to this conviction under the influence of his personality and ministry.

Only in a few of the later books of the New Testament does the
argument based on the fulfillment of specific prophecies occupy a
prominent place. In the books written by Paul, in the early sermons
in Acts and in Mark's Gospel the emphasis is on the fulfillment of
all Scripture, and very few passages quote a specific prophecy of the
Old Testament.

Paul was convinced that the gospel was in accord with the Old
Testament revelation. He justified the Gentile mission by an appeal to several Old Testament passages, such as Ps. 18:49, Deut.
32:43, Ps. 117:1, and Isa. 11:10 (Rom. 15:9-12). He did not

say specifically that it was the fulfillment of those Old Testament passages; the implication was rather that the passages showed that preaching the gospel to all the Gentiles was in accordance with God's purpose and was taking place now in accordance with his will. He used the same argument in Romans 9-11, and quoted Isa. 59:20-21 and Jer. 31:33 to show that all Israel would be saved (Rom. 11:26-27). What Paul really does in such passages is to present the gospel in the context of the whole Old Testament revelation. On the other hand, he never quotes any specific passages from the Old Testament in connection with his interpretation of the death and resurrection of Jesus. He asserts that the gospel was "promised beforehand through his prophets in the holy scriptures," a reference to all Scripture. "The law and the prophets" witness to the righteousness of God revealed now in Christ, because the Old Testament is also a revelation of the grace of God. Paul reads the Old Testament, not from the legalistic point of view of what God demands of man, but rather as a revelation of what God has done and will do for man's salvation. For that reason "the promise," or "the promises," is to him the central message of the Old Testament. Grace, promise, faith are the great realities of the Old Testament, and these have now come to humanity in full measure through Christ. The salvation in Christ is "according to the Scriptures," but from his point of view this conviction requires neither legalistic casuistry nor arguments from the fulfillment of specific prophecies. To Paul, the gospel was primarily an event to be proclaimed, not a proposition to be proved.

In the chapters in Acts which describe the early church there are some references to specific fulfillment of prophecy, although the specific formula is not used. The betrayal of Jesus was regarded as having been foretold in Ps. 69:25 and 109:8 (Acts 1:20). On the basis of the prophecy, the apostles and the church selected another to take Judas' place. In Acts 2:17-21, Peter appealed to Joel 2:28-32 in order to explain what had happened on the day of Pentecost. This quotation is very interesting and instructive for our understanding of the thinking of the early church. On the one hand, if Peter really meant that the prophecy from Joel, which speaks of what is to happen "in the last days" and on "the day of the Lord," was being fulfilled in his own time, he must have thought of the event of Christ as final, and he must have included the return of Christ from heaven. Obviously the reference to the signs and wonders when "the sun shall be turned into darkness and the moon into blood" cannot refer to the day of Pentecost. Peter's selecting this quotation then would clearly indicate that the disciples thought of the Crucifixion, the Resurrection, the Ascension, the outpouring of the Spirit, *and the Return* as one event which was taking place in their time: this was the end and all the prophecies were being fulfilled. On the other hand, it is possible that we have here an example of how loosely and nonchalantly the Apostles quoted from the Old Testament. In quoting long passages they were not necessarily implying that all the parts of the quotation were to be applied to the matter in hand. Possibly in this instance Peter was primarily interested in the first and the last part of the prophecy, the outpouring of the Spirit, and "whoever calls on the name of the Lord shall be saved," the points emphasized in his speech on this occasion. The first of these alternatives, however, seems to be closest to the thinking of the early church.

In the sermons in Acts we find only a few direct quotations from the Old Testament. The enmity Jesus had met and their own sufferings reminded the disciples of the words of Ps. 2:1-2 (Acts 4:25-26), the Resurrection, of Ps. 16:8-11 (Acts 2:25-28) and 132:11 (Acts 2:30), and the Ascension, of Ps. 110:1 (Acts 2:34-35). Chapter 2 of Acts is the only passage in the New Testament that quotes an Old Testament prophecy in connection with the Resurrection. (This is of course quite understandable since no writer in the Old Testament had conceived of the Messiah as dying and rising again.) Rather than citing specific prophecies, the sermons in Acts reiterate again and again that what has happened in the event of Christ is in accordance with the Scriptures and the purpose of God.

The Gospel of Mark has only a few quotations from the Old

Testament, and only once is it implied that a specific prophecy has
been fulfilled. The appearance of John the Baptist is connected
with Mal. 3:1 and Isa. 40:3 (Mark 1:2-3). That Jesus spoke in
parables is explained by his reference to Isa. 6:9-10 (Mark 4:12).
In Mark 7:6, Jesus says that Isaiah "prophesied concerning you
hypocrites," and in 12:10 he refers to "the stone which the build-
ers rejected" (Ps. 118:22). Psalm 110:1 is quoted in connection
with the question of the Messiah's being the son of David (Mark
12:36). In none of these passages is it suggested that these prophecies were fulfilled in the events concerned.

The only passage in Mark which specifically asserts that a prophecy has been fulfilled is found in 14:27: "You will all fall away;
for it is written, 'I will strike the shepherd, and the sheep will be
scattered'" (Zech. 13:7). The formula is lacking, however, and
it is perhaps significant that this quotation occurs in the passion
story, which in all the Gospels is filled with allusions to the Old
Testament. The one formula quotation in Mark, 15:28, "and the
scripture was fulfilled which says, 'He was reckoned with the trans-
gressors,'" is not accepted as a genuine part of the Gospel text. The
insertion of that kind of a quotation in the text of Mark indicates
a later tendency in the church to find specific prophecies that Jesus
fulfilled.

The quotations we have noted here illustrate the way the New
Testament people used the Old Testament in their preaching. When
Paul used Old Testament passages to justify the Gentile mission, he
was using it in the same way a modern preacher uses passages from
the Bible to reinforce or illustrate a point he wants to make. Paul
was not concerned to show that his mission fulfilled certain prophecies, but he was anxious to demonstrate that his mission was in
accordance with the plan and purpose of God. Most of the use of
the Old Testament in the New comes in this category.

It is in the two later Gospels, Matthew and John, that we find
the emphasis on the fulfillment of specific prophecies. Here we
find the definite formula *hina plerothe,* "in order that it might be
fulfilled," or *tote eplerothe,* "thus was fulfilled." There are many

passages in Matthew where the formula is used and a specific prophecy is quoted: e.g., 1:22; 2:15,17,23; 4:14; 8:17; 13:35; 21:4; 27:9. In addition, there are two passages where it is said that "the scriptures" are fulfilled: "But all this has taken place that the scriptures of the prophets might be fulfilled" (26:56), and "How then should the scriptures be fulfilled" (26:54). Other passages clearly imply that a specific prophecy must be fulfilled. When Herod asked where the Christ was to be born, the priests and the scribes cited Mic. 5:2 to indicate Bethlehem (Matt. 2:5). John the Baptist was identified as the one Isaiah had spoken of both by the evangelist (3:3) and by Jesus (11:10). According to Matthew, as to Mark, Jesus' speaking in parables is a fulfillment of the prophecy of Isaiah (Matt. 13:14-15). In each of these passages a specific prophecy is cited, with the implication that it is now fulfilled.

In the Gospel of John there are several passages in which the same formula is used (12:38, 13:18, 15:25, 19:24, 19:28, 19:36). With some variations in the formula, in each case it is pointed out that a certain incident fulfills a specific word of prophecy. According to John's record, Jesus asserted that the defection of Judas took place "that the scripture might be fulfilled," an allusion to Ps. 41:9 (John 17:12). There are also two passages in which words previously spoken by Jesus are said to be fulfilled: "Of those whom thou gavest me I lost not one" (18:9), and the word predicting the manner of his death (18:32). In 6:45 Jesus quotes Isa. 54:13, "they shall all be taught by God," with the implication that the prophecy is now fulfilled in his teaching. Some other quotations or allusions to the Old Testament (John 1:23; 2:17; 6:31; 7:42; 12:13,15) suggest fulfillment of prophecies without specifically stating it.

Luke does not employ the formula, and he gives very few examples of the fulfillment of prophecy. He has Jesus himself assert that the words of Isaiah which he read in the synagogue of Nazareth are "today ... fulfilled in your hearing" (Luke 4:21), but the passage refers to the whole ministry and mission of Jesus. These words from Isaiah stand in Luke's Gospel as a kind of a text which

the rest of the Gospel elucidates. The whole Gospel may be regarded as an exposition of them. This was the type of ministry
which Jesus had come to fulfill. Luke's Gospel is an exposition of
the faith of the church that Jesus fulfilled the whole purpose of
God as revealed in the Old Testament. The great hymns in chapters 1 and 2 emphasize this general fulfillment.

### JESUS' FULFILLMENT OF GOD'S PURPOSE

What significant conclusions can be drawn on the basis of this
difference in emphasis between the fulfillment of all Scripture and
the fulfillment of specific prophecies?

In the first place, it is significant that the practice of pointing to
the fulfillment of specific prophecies is found generally in the later
books of the New Testament, such as Matthew and John. Paul,
Mark, and for the most part the sermons in Acts do not use this
device. In these works we find instead an emphasis on the general
fulfillment of God's "counsel and purpose" as recorded "in the
Scriptures." This was evidently the faith in Jesus with which
those in the early church began. Since they believed in the general
fulfillment of God's purpose in the event of Christ, it is quite understandable that later, applying this faith to individual passages
in the Old Testament, they would begin to cite specific prophecies
fulfilled by Jesus. The later books of the New Testament show
that as time went on this appeal to prophecy became so general
that a stereotyped formula came to be used to introduce the quotation.

In the second place, it is clear that something else besides a late
date determined the use of this argument from prophecy. The Gospel of Luke was written at about the same time as the Gospel of
Matthew, and the Fourth Gospel was written shortly afterwards.
But Luke does not use this mode of quotation. Why is it that this
method of quoting Scripture is confined to the two Gospels of
Matthew and John?

In a recent study of Matthew's Gospel, Krister Stendahl has
shown that the First Gospel is the product of a school rather than

of one man. His inquiry deals with the *Sitz-im-Leben* ("creative milieu") of the Gospel, which he suggests is not to be found in the preaching of the early church (as held by Dibelius), nor in liturgical practice (Kilpatrick), nor in catechetical instruction (C. H. Dodd), but in a more highly developed school environment. "The systematizing work, the adaptation toward casuistry instead of broad statements of principles, the reflection on the position of the church leaders and their duties, and many other similar features, all point to a milieu of study and instruction."[2] Whoever wrote the First Gospel, it shows the influence of a school environment in which definite methods of study, research, systematization, and instruction had been developed.

It has long been recognized that John's Gospel also comes from a school environment. The twenty-first chapter suggests definitely that other men were associated with the author, even though the question whether the Gospel is a composite work or the product of one man may be left open. It may be assumed, however, that the author was the leader of a group, a school, or a *chaburah*,[3] which had developed a distinct interpretation of the significance of Jesus. Stendahl suggests that Matthew's Gospel is also the product of a school, and that it is "a manual of discipline and a catechism of Christian behavior" which is to serve the church leaders as well as the general constituency. The greater part of Stendahl's work is devoted to showing that the formula quotations and the treatment of the Old Testament prove his contention that the Gospel originated in "the school of St. Matthew."

Luke's Gospel, on the contrary, is the work of one man, a historical and literary artist who wanted to "set forth in order the things which have been fulfilled among us." He records the events and the proclamation and interpretation of the gospel preachers who proclaim "the mighty works of God." His work is more immediately related to the original faith and to the preaching tradition of the church. So A. B. Bruce remarks about the two evange-

---

[2] Krister Stendahl, *The School of St. Matthew* (Uppsala, 1954), p. 29.
[3] Anton J. Fridrichsen, "Epilog," in *Svensk Exegetisk Årsbok* (1948), p. 123.

lists' versions of the Sermon on the Mount: "In Matthew it is
*didache,* in Luke *kerygma.*"[4]

If Stendahl's analysis is correct, it helps us to explain the prominence of the argument from prophecy in the Gospels of Matthew
and John. Such a method and procedure belongs in the school
rather than in the general proclamation of the gospel. It is the
product of study and reflection, which we would expect to arise
later as the need for a more detailed exposition of the Christian
faith developed. The apologist and the instructor can use the
casuistry of the argument from the fulfillment of prophecy to good
advantage. They need to cite authority and give reasons why the
gospel should be accepted, whereas a gospel preacher like Paul
proclaims the message of God's marvelous work in the event of
Christ and urges men to repentance and faith. It was in the school
environment, then, that the type of exegesis represented by the
formula quotations in the Gospels of Matthew and John arose, as
a later development on the basis of the original faith in Jesus as
the Fulfiller of God's promises and his purpose. The later approach
did not replace the earlier; the church continued to emphasize both.

In the third place, it must be pointed out that the argument from
the fulfillment of prophecy became even more prominent in the
later church. The teachers of the church vied with one another in
finding specific passages in the Old Testament which could be made
to point to Jesus. The typological method of interpretation became
very popular, and the results achieved were sometimes a little
strange. Barnabas possibly reaches the point of *reductio ad absur-
dum* when he suggests that the number 318 of those who helped
Abraham rescue Lot (Gen. 14:14) was a type of Jesus and the
cross (Barnabas IX, 8). Clement declares that the scarlet cord in
the window of Rahab (Josh. 2:18) foreshadowed redemption in
the blood of Christ (Clement XII, 7). Such exegesis flourishes
even today, and the ingenuity which is shown in finding prophetic
types in the Old Testament is really remarkable.

---

[4]*The Expositor's Greek New Testament,* ed. W. Robertson Nicoll (2nd ed.,
New York, 1901), I, 504.

In comparison with these later exaggerations the schools of Matthew and John were rather conservative. Their conception of prophecy was not as atomistic and mechanical as has sometimes been assumed. After all, they started with and shared the common conviction that Jesus fulfilled all Scripture. When they quote a specific passage, the larger context must be taken into consideration. Even such a specific reference as "Out of Egypt have I called my son" may not be as far-fetched as it seems, for it recalled to the early Christians the whole history and imagery of the redemption out of Egypt, to which the gospel formed a certain analogy.

In the fourth place, we are left with the impression that the argument from the fulfillment of prophecy, i.e., the fulfillment of specific prophecies, was not as prominent in the early church as has sometimes been assumed. The whole New Testament bears witness to the faith that Jesus fulfilled the plan and purpose of God, but the use of individual and specific prophecies is limited almost entirely to the Gospels of Matthew and John. The early Christians used the Old Testament in their interpretation of the new event of Christ, but the idea that they hunted around in it for passages that would correspond to certain events in the life of Jesus, and that this was the basis of their faith, is a misinterpretation.

A theory has long been in vogue that the first literary production of the early church was a collection of "testimonies," i.e., a collection of Old Testament prophecies which the disciples interpreted as being fulfilled in Christ. This theory was first suggested by Rendel Harris, and it has become quite generally accepted. C. H. Dodd comes to the conclusion, however, that the evidence for such a collection is very weak.[5] If such a collection was ever made and circulated freely in the church, it is strange that it has left no appreciable trace in the writings of Mark, Luke, and Paul. The reference to "books and parchments" in II Tim. 4:13 probably concerns Old Testament books. Furthermore, the early Christian preachers were quite well acquainted with the Old Testament, especially with the

---

[5] C. H. Dodd, *According to the Scriptures* (New York, 1953), p. 26.

Pentateuch, Psalms, Isaiah, and Jeremiah. (These are the books most frequently quoted in the New Testament.[6]) They did not need a special collection of proof texts. The freedom with which New Testament writers used the Old Testament both in allusions and quotations leads us to conclude rather that they often quoted from memory and that they interpreted the event of Christ in the broad perspective of the whole purpose of God as revealed in the Old Testament.[7] That Jesus fulfilled "all Scripture" was the common conviction of those who had experienced the miracles of Easter and Pentecost.

On the basis of this faith, however, it would be natural for them to begin to see in the life of Jesus and especially in the passion story certain parallels and analogies with the events and words of these sacred Scriptures. This would be true especially later when the Christians began to reflect on their faith and to express it in more systematic forms. The Scriptures were to them God's word and his revelation of himself and his purpose. The Christians were now the people of God, and heirs to all that God had said and done in the past. The new event which they saw happening was to them the fulfillment of all that God had spoken. They were free, therefore, to use the Old Testament as a part of their proclamation and to show that God's eternal purpose was now fulfilled in Christ. Their faith, however, was founded on Jesus and on *all* the Scriptures. They did not show any need of finding a foundation for their faith in precarious interpretations of typology and prophecy.

Finally, it must be realized that fulfillment, whether of "the Scriptures" or individual prophecies, is never simply a reproduction of the old, but a new development and a new event. "Out of Egypt have I called my son" was true for the New Testament people in an entirely different setting. Although they could find analogies in the past, the present event was new. The center of their faith was in the passion story, in the death and resurrection of Jesus. Since

----

[6]*Ibid.*, pp. 61 ff.

[7]For a detailed study of the problem, see Dodd, *op. cit.;* Stendahl, *op. cit.;* and E. Earl Ellis, *Paul's Use of the Old Testament* (Edinburgh, 1957).

he was the chosen and anointed of God and the living Lord, the whole of God's revelation had its center in him. The Old Testament is not the source of the Christian faith; it is a witness to and a help in the interpretation of the life and work of Jesus. The event of Christ was "according to the Scriptures," but the fulfillment was a new act of God that transcended everything that had gone before.

## JESUS' FULFILLMENT OF THE LAW

In a few passages in the Gospels, Jesus says that he has come, not "to abolish the law and the prophets, but to fulfill them" (Matt. 5:17; cf. Luke 16:17). This fulfillment of the law has been incorporated into the doctrine of the atonement in the sense that Jesus fulfilled the law in our stead. Since sinful humanity could not fulfill the law, and since the law of God had to be fulfilled by man, the God-man Jesus Christ fulfilled it for all. This aspect of the law will be discussed in a different context, but it may be said here that no passage in the New Testament can be made to say he fulfilled the law for us. It is of course true that all his life was vicarious and that he came into this world *for us*. The New Testament writers assert not only that he was sinless but also that he lived a life of perfect obedience to God. That was a part of his mission and work. At this point we are interested in asking in what sense Jesus may be said to have fulfilled the law.

The Hebrew word which we translate "law" is *torah,* which really means direction, instruction, and hence revelation. God's torah is the revelation of himself and his purpose. In the Old Testament the word frequently stands for the whole revelation of God.

The psalmist praises the torah as his dearest possessions. "[The righteous man's] delight is in the law of the Lord, and on his law he meditates day and night" (Ps. 1:2). "The law is my delight" (119:77). "I long for thy salvation, O Lord, and thy law is my delight" (119:174). It would be an injustice to the psalmist to interpret "law" here in a legalistic sense. What he is celebrating is the love, mercy, and grace of the Lord revealed to him in God's dealings with his people.

In the same way the prophets use "law" in a wide sense to refer to God's grace and revelation. "Hear the word of the Lord, you rulers of Sodom! Give ear to the teaching [*torah*] of our God, you people of Gomorrah" (Isa.1:10). "Out of Zion shall go forth the law, and the word of the Lord from Jerusalem" (2:3). In these passages "the word of the Lord" and "the law" are synonomous. When the prophet says that "the coastlands wait for his law" (42:4), he certainly does not mean that they are waiting just for the commandments and ordinances which we might understand as we read the word law. What they are waiting for is the revelation of himself that God has given to Israel to carry to the ends of the earth. It would be truer to the meaning of the prophet if we substituted the word "gospel" in these passages. "The coastlands wait for his gospel," the good news of the new age which the returning exiles were to proclaim in all the world.

When the prophets denounce the people for transgressing the law, the transgression is a question of attitude, not merely of breaking a few commandments. "They have rejected the law of the Lord of hosts" (Isa. 5:24). "They have rejected the law of the Lord" (Amos 2:4). "[They] have forsaken me and have not kept my law" (Jer. 16:11). This attitude is apostasy, rebellion, unbelief, and indifference to God: the people have rejected the torah in which God has revealed himself as their Lord and Savior.

Since the writers of the New Testament regarded the Old Testament as the Word of God, and since almost all of them were bilingual, using both Hebrew and Greek, we would expect the Old Testament usage to be reflected in the vocabulary of the New. When they used the Greek word *nomos* ("law") for the term *torah,* the Hebrew connotation of the word translated should lie close at hand, and indeed, we do find that in many passages in the New Testament the word *nomos* must be understood in the wider sense of torah rather than law in a strict sense. In several instances quotations from the psalms and the prophets are introduced by the formula, "it is written in the law." Thus in John 10:34, Jesus says, "Is it not written in your law, 'I said, you are gods'?" alluding to Ps. 82:6. After Paul has grouped together a number of quotations in Rom. 3:10-19, mostly from the psalms, he concludes: "Whatever the law says it speaks to those who are under the law." Similarly in I Cor. 14:21 Paul uses the expression "in the law it is written," although the quotation introduced is from Isaiah (28:11-12). In John 15:25, Jesus says that the Jews "fulfilled the word written in their law, 'They hated me without a cause'" (Ps. 35:19). When the Jews say, "We have heard from the law that the Christ remains for ever" (John 12:34), they are thinking of the messianic prophecies in the Old Testament.

In these passages it is evident that "law" stands for the Scriptures, or for the whole Old Testament. Since the Pentateuch was the fundamental document of Israel's existence as a people, and since these books stood first in the canon, it was quite natural to refer to this collection as the Torah. In addition, since the fundamental meaning of torah is direction or revelation, it could very well be said, "it is written in the Torah," when quoting from any part of the Old Testament.

It is necessary, therefore, to examine the passages in which *nomos* occurs in the New Testament in order to determine whether they refer to law in the strict sense of the word, or whether they refer to the Torah as the revelation, the Scriptures. The distinction which Paul makes in Romans and Galatians between "the righteousness by the law" and "the righteousness from God" is not a distinction between the Old and the New Testaments. The issue here is legalism versus freedom, salvation of self by self versus salvation by grace. Paul had to struggle with the Judaizers who insisted that the way of salvation was by obedience to the commandments—at least, that is the way Paul interprets their stand. The word law, then, does not stand here for the Torah as the Old Testament Scriptures. We could express what Paul had in mind here by the Reformation differentiation between "law" and "gospel." However, this distinction ought not to determine the interpretation of passages in which this issue is not present. When Stephen and later Paul are accused of "speaking against the law," it is a question of their interpretation of the whole Old Testament. When Paul speaks of "those who have sinned without the law" and "those who have sinned under the law," he is really making a comparison between the Gentiles, who do not have the revelation, and the Jews, who possess the Old Testament. *Nomos* here refers to the whole Old Testament, in its aspects as law and as gospel, and Paul would insist that grace, promise, gospel, is primary in it.

When Jesus says, "Think not that I have come to abolish the law and the prophets; I have come not to abolish them but to fulfil them" (Matt. 5:17), he is simply asserting that he has come to accomplish God's purpose of redemption revealed in the Scriptures. The meaning must be the same in the next statement when he says: "For truly, I say to you, till heaven and earth pass away, not an iota, not a dot, will pass from the law until all is accomplished" (5:18). Since verse 17 has "the law and the prophets," "the law" in verse 18 must have the same meaning: the Torah as the whole Old Testament. This must be true also of the parallel passage in Luke 16:17: "But it is easier for heaven and earth to pass away, than for one dot of the law to become void," for here, too, the verse immediately preceding has "law and prophets." Jesus is not here subscribing to the rabbinical tendency to exalt the laws, regulations, and ordinances, both oral and written, to the status of divine permanence. As Hunter says, "The doctrine of the law's permanence is pure Rabbinism, and Jesus himself relaxed the Sabbath law, annulled the law about purity, and rejected Moses' commandment about divorce."[8] He argues that Jesus could not have subscribed to the idea that all the commandments were permanently binding. What was eternally binding was the Torah as the revelation of God's purpose and will. If we understand law here in that sense, the doctrine of the permanence of the law as revelation is thoroughly Christian and in accordance with the teaching of the New Testament as a whole.

---

[8]Archibald M. Hunter, *A Pattern for Life* (Philadelphia, 1953), p. 43.

What Jesus asserts, therefore, as he speaks of the law, is that "the Scriptures must be fulfilled," that not the smallest detail of God's plan shall be left undone, and that the promises of God to his people shall be kept in their entirety. God is the God of faithfulness and steadfast love. Jesus further declares that he knows himself to be the agent through whom this purpose of God shall be accomplished. "I have come not to abolish the law and the prophets," i.e., not to act contrary to what God has already revealed, "I have come to fulfil." He knows that he stands in a long context of God's redemptive activity which embraces everything from the creation to the consummation. All that God has revealed and promised will be fulfilled. The early church believed that Jesus fulfilled all Scripture, and this belief was evidently based on what Jesus himself had said about his ministry and mission.

### THE NATURE OF PROPHECY AND FULFILLMENT

Prophecy is a proclamation and an interpretation of God's acts in history. Such biblical events as those we have analyzed in the second chapter are the raw material with which the prophet deals. He proclaims these events to remind the people of what God has done in their history, and he interprets them for the present generation. Since the three factors in these events are judgment, redemption, and promise, the prophetic proclamation is also concerned with these three factors.

The event cannot be interpreted until after it has occurred. God must act in order to provide the basic revelation of himself. "In the Bible the rule stands that God's acts must actually take place before new terms can be coined."[9] Conversely, when the act has occurred new thoughts can now be proclaimed. When the event has taken place, it is the task of the prophet to interpret its meaning to the people.

It is rather obvious that this is the sequence followed in the Bible. When the Exodus has taken place, Moses can interpret its

---

[9] Wingren, *op. cit.,* p. 43.

meaning to the people. God has chosen them by this act of redemption to be his own. Since they are now his people by virtue of this act of redemption, they are to live as his people, worshiping him and serving him in obedience to his will. The fact that God has redeemed them is stated again and again in the Pentateuch. God has chosen them in grace and mercy for his own sake, not because of any greatness or honor on their part. They are to remember this act and tell it to succeeding generations, because this is the act that has established them as the people of God. It is not their obedience to the law that makes them his people, nor anything else that they may do or possess. He is "the faithful God who keeps covenant and steadfast love with those who love him and keep his commandments" (Deut. 7:9). They have been chosen because "the Lord loves you, and is keeping the oath which he swore to your fathers" (7:8). Their whole history and their conception of themselves as a people are predicated on this act of God. This is the prophetic interpretation of the Exodus event.

The same interpretation is to be found in the prophets and the psalms. Over and over again we hear the refrain that God has led their fathers out of the house of bondage and has made them his people. "In the sight of their fathers he wrought marvels in the land of Egypt, in the fields of Zoan" (Ps. 78:12). "Thou didst bring thy people Israel out of the land of Egypt with signs and wonders, with a strong hand and outstretched arm, and with great terror, and thou gavest them this land" (Jer. 32:21-22). The prophet interprets God's action. On the basis of what God has done the prophet calls on the people to respect the covenant, to worship the Lord and to trust in him alone. Isaiah's parable of the vineyard is typical of the prophet's approach. God has done everything for his people. He has poured out his grace and blessings on them from the call of Abraham to the prophet's own day. He urges them to give up trusting in their own strength, or in foreign alliances, and to return to faith in "the God of the covenant and steadfast love."

The return from the Exile had to be an assured fact before the prophetic vision of this event could be interpreted. Up to that time the event could be promised, but no final interpretation was possible. On the basis of this new creative and redemptive act of God the prophet envisions a new age. As God led their fathers out of Egypt, so now he is preparing a highway for the return of the exiles to Jerusalem. This is a new act of God, a new event. It is not to be a repetition of the old story of a faithless people. They will become the witnesses to all the world of God's redemptive work, and the prophet proclaims and interprets the event which is now taking place.

In the New Testament the death and resurrection of Jesus had to take place before it could be proclaimed and interpreted. There is a remarkable lack of interpretation of the death of Jesus in the Gospels.[10] His death is predicted three times in practically the same words. "He began to teach them that the Son of man must suffer many things, and be rejected by the elders and the chief priests and the scribes, and be killed, and after three days rise again" (Mark 8:31; cf. 9:31, 10:33). Various other hints are given, and at least one specific statement: "The Son of man also came not to be served but to serve, and to give his life as a ransom for many" (10:45). The disciples found it very difficult to accept this pronouncement, and they wondered what it could mean that the Son of man should rise from the dead (9:9-10). The Resurrection was not a part of their messianic expectation. Peter's reaction to the announcement was quite natural: "God forbid, Lord! This shall never happen to you" (Matt. 16:22).

When the event has taken place, a new word and a new message can be proclaimed. The return from the Exile was not the reconstitution of the old Israel, it was a new creation, a new people of God. After the Resurrection, the Ascension, and Pentecost the disciples could proclaim that Christ "was delivered for our transgres-

---

[10]Cf. Vincent Taylor, *Jesus and His Sacrifice* (London, 1951). Taylor examines all the passages in the Synoptic Gospels that allude to Jesus' death, but it is quite obvious that these are allusions and predictions, not interpretations. John's Gospel, which is written from the retrospective point of view of faith in the risen Lord, can provide more interpretation of his death, as for example in chapter 6. In the Synoptic Gospels his death is announced and predicted, but the real interpretation follows after the event.

sions and raised for our justification." His coming was not merely
the fulfillment of the Jewish messianic hope and of the various
conceptions of the Messiah which had developed through the centuries. In the fusion of the three concepts—Son of man, Suffering
Servant, Messiah—a new revelation was given which was greater
than the sum total of the three factors. Jesus Christ cannot be adequately interpreted by a mere combination of these three concepts.
He not only combined them, he gave them a new and deeper significance. The apostolic message is different even from the teaching
of Jesus, because only after the event could the real interpretation
of his work be made.[11] After his death and the Resurrection the
church understood that this event was a redemptive act of God,
and that through this tragic suffering God had prepared a way of
salvation for all the world. The Cross had been a stumbling block,
a *skandalon,* even to the disciples, but now they knew that it was
"the power of God and the wisdom of God."

Prophecy, therefore, does not reveal history, not even redemptive
history, in advance. The living God who is the sovereign Lord fulfills his promises in his own time and in his own way. Just as Jesus
did not conform to the popular, messianic expectation, so any attempt on our part to decide when and how the next event is to
take place is doomed to failure. The Parousia is a promise, not a
blueprint of the future. It remains true that the event has to happen
before it can be interpreted. *After* an event men can look back, as
the early church did, and see certain correspondencies between what
has been said and done in the past and what has now occurred. But
up to the time the event happens it remains a promise whose fulfillment God himself determines in accordance with his purpose. It
can be proclaimed as a promise, and the fulfillment may be pictured
in various forms, but essentially it remains a promise to be fulfilled
by God, who is the God "of the covenant and of steadfast love."

The prophet is not concerned primarily with the future but with

---

[11]"The proclamation of Jesus and the *kerygma* of the church are by no means
identical, but neither are they incompatible" (Reginald H. Fuller, *The Mission
and Achievement of Jesus* [Chicago, 1954], p. 117).

the relationship of God to his own generation; ie., the event of the past and its implications for the present. The eighth-century prophets were trying to bring Israel back to trust in and obedience to Yahweh, and they reminded the people, therefore, of what God had done in the past, especially in the Exodus. Isaiah was concerned with the problems that confronted King Ahaz and his people. He tried to persuade them to trust in God. If they wanted to be "established," they must believe in the sign to be given them, a child whose name would be "Immanuel," God with us. Matthew sees this sign being fulfilled in a much more real sense in the birth of Christ, for "God was in Christ," but Isaiah was not concerned about this distant future. He was interested simply in bringing Ahaz and his people back to faith and trust in Yahweh. The prophets of the Exile likewise reminded the people of God's merciful acts toward his people in the past in order that they might now believe and accept the task of being the bearers of God's revelation to all the world. The sermons in Acts and the missionary preaching of Paul were designed to bring people to faith in the gospel. The purpose of the Gospel of John and of the whole New Testament is "that you may believe that Jesus is the Christ, the Son of God, and that believing you may have life in his name" (John 20:31). Thus the preachers of the gospel interpreted the act of God in Christ to their own contemporaries.

This prophetic message, in spite of the new elements added to it by each succeeding event, is in a certain sense always the same. It is the simple message that God seeks man, comes to man, meets him, and confronts him. In this sense there is no essential difference between God's coming to Adam and Eve and his coming to us in Christ. To stand before God means to be confronted with judgment, redemption, and a promise. Whether the preacher be Noah, Isaiah, Paul or a contemporary, the message is the same: repent, believe, hope. When a man believes, he believes in the reality and the relevancy of this act of God for him. Abraham believed God, the God "who gives life to the dead and calls into existence the things that do not exist" (Rom. 4:17). The event itself is

judgment, redemption, and promise, and the response of those who
hear this message is repentance, faith, and hope. The object of
faith is the redemptive act of God in the past, and the object of
hope is the promise of a future event. The office and task of the
prophet is always the same, whether he belonged in the Old Testament, in the New, or is a contemporary witness to the revelation of
God in Christ.

Since prophecy is concerned with the acts of God, it is always related to his redemptive purpose. In consequence, the biblical writers are not concerned with the prognosis of world history as such.
The Bible furnishes no answer to such questions as the outcome of
"the cold war." Such world rulers as Attila, Napoleon, Hitler,
and Stalin are not to be found within its pages. Since the Bible is
concerned with sin and redemption, different ages may recognize
themselves in a situation parallel to the conflict between God and
the powers of evil described in various places in the Bible, but
Scripture is not concerned with secular history as such. The kingdom which it proclaims is not a political or national entity; it is the
eternal kingdom which God himself establishes. Political prognos-
ticators of utopian schemes may use biblical material, but they are
not prophets of God. The prophet's task is to confront man with
the Word of the Lord and to interpret the significance of his acts
to the world. Although in doing so a true prophet may have a great
deal to say about the social, political, economic, and moral life in
the contemporary scene, what he has to say is on the basis of what
God has done in the past and is doing in the present, not on the
basis of some occult blueprint for world history contained in the
Bible.

## PROMISE AND HOPE

Since the acts of God, the events, are not only judgment and redemption but also a promise, the prophet cannot avoid speaking
about the future. When he does so he is not gazing into some crystal
ball that reveals to him the specific course of history in advance. He
is interpreting God's intention and purpose on the basis of God's

acts in the past. He reads the meaning of the future out of the events which have already taken place. Actually, the promise is already involved in the event that has taken place, or is taking place, and is an integral part of it. When Israel leaves Egypt, it is for the purpose of going to the promised land. The exiles return to rebuild Jerusalem. In the New Testament kerygma this future element is supplied by the hope of the return of Christ. Since he is the Victor over death, the "last enemy" will be destroyed (I Cor. 15:26). Faith in the risen and living Lord would be unthinkable apart from the hope that "he shall reign for ever and ever" (Rev. 11:15). Even though the early Christians thought of the return as a part of the present event, they nevertheless expected an interval between the Ascension and the return. They waited for him "whom heaven must receive until the time for establishing all that God spoke by the mouth of his holy prophets from of old" (Acts 3:21). Whether the interval was thought of in terms of a longer or shorter period makes no essential difference. When men asked, "Where is the promise of his coming?" the answer to that skeptical question had to be found in the event that had already taken place, the event of the Cross and the Resurrection. But without the faith in a final consummation, the whole biblical perspective would become meaningless.

The Christian hope in the final triumph of God's kingdom is, therefore, primarily and fundamentally a hope in God. It has nothing to do with calculations about the probable length of this age, nor with the possibility that the energy of the sun will abruptly diminish, nor with any other possible cataclysmic event in nature or history that may put an end to human existence on the earth. The Christian hope concerning a meaningful end of the history of our creation rests firmly on the promise implied and given in the events of the past and in God's activity in the present. Its foundation for the individual Christian is a personal relationship to him "who loved me and gave himself for me." No one has expressed this better than John does when he says: "Beloved, we are God's children now; it does not yet appear what we shall be, but we know that when he appears we shall be like him, for we shall see him as he is. And every one who thus hopes in him purifies himself as he is pure" (I John 3:2-3). Here past, present, and future are united in one vast reality which spans both time and eternity.

It was inevitable that the New Testament writers should express this hope in apocalyptic imagery familiar to the people of their own time. All the acts of God are cosmic and eschatological events in which the Creator deals with his creation. They thought of the planets, sun and moon as being involved in the drama. The future event, the climax of the whole series, would involve the totality of God's creation. "Then I saw a great white throne and him who sat upon it; from his presence earth and sky fled away, and no place was found for them" (Rev. 20:11). Since the whole work of God is presented in the Bible as a great conflict between God and the evil powers, it is inevitable that the end should be conceived of in terms of a great victory which brings these powers to nought and establishes God's eternal kingdom. Just as faith speaks of the work of God in the past in metaphors of ransom or liberation or new birth, so hope may speak in extravagant and fanciful figures of the work of God that is yet to come. The early church used the common apocalyptic figures to express this hope. Not all these figures need be interpreted. Some of them are unintelligible to us. What the figures express is the common conviction of the Christians that Jesus is the fulfillment of all the promises of God, and that "he who began a good work in you will bring it to completion at the day of Jesus Christ" (Phil. 1:6). The church did not regard it as an idle boast when Jesus said: "All authority in heaven and on earth has been given to me" (Matt. 28:18). Jubilantly she confessed: "He shall reign for ever and ever." This is the prophetic message of the Christian hope.

The Christian hope today is essentially the same in meaning as the hope that has been held and expressed by the people of all ages within the biblical record. Man always stands in the same situation between the events of the past and the promise. The content of the promise may be conceived of differently in different periods. Israel hoped to take possession of the land and establish a strong nation. The hope of the saints has often been for vengeance upon their enemies. But such aims are hardly compatible with the event of Christ. In the final analysis the hope is in God. He will "make all things new," but what that really means is hidden in his eternal counsel and purpose.

Christian hope is neither the negation nor the abolition of history. As long as we believe that God works in history, we must take the historical process seriously. In a very real sense our hope concerns the fulfillment of history, for the historical process is God's work. The realization of his purpose and plans is not a repudiation of the past, but its fulfillment. While each of the key events was a new act of God, it did not negate the past. The past was taken up into the new event and received a larger and more significant meaning. As all the events have been acts of redemption, so that event to which hope looks forward is also a redemptive event. "Now when these things begin to take place, look up and raise your heads, because your redemption is drawing near" (Luke 21:28).

The character and nature of this hope are determined, therefore, by the character and nature of God's acts in the past, pre-eminently the event of Christ. The Christian hope has its center in him. It is he who shall return and establish his kingdom. Because he is Jesus, the crucified and risen Lord, we can look forward confidently to his return. "Jesus Christ is the same yesterday and today and for ever" (Heb. 13:8). On that last day we do not meet a stranger. We meet "the same Person whose holiness, truth and love we already know in Christ; and if we have to 'appear before the judgment seat of Christ,' we may believe that the sign of the cross will be over all."[12]

We do not empty the Christian hope of its content by this interpretation. To be sure, we recognize the apocalyptic imagery for what it is, the product of an age which expressed its faith in vivid pictures and images drawn from oriental courts and given cosmic

---

[12]Hunter, *Interpreting Paul's Gospel* (Philadelphia, 1955), p. 130.

proportions. We, too, may even use these figures. The city of God, the kingdom of God, the great white throne, the Lamb that was slain are all figures from the experiences of our life. The essential content is not the figures themselves; it is the crucified and risen Lord. Our whole conception of the Christian hope must be drawn from him who "came that we may have life, and have it abundantly."

# 4.

# The Event of Christ

Since the church refused to follow the lead of Marcion in rejecting the Old Testament, the event of Christ has always been seen in the context of the whole Bible, and his coming has been interpreted as the fulfillment of Old Testament prophecy. The God who sent Jesus into the world is the same God as the God of creation, of Abraham, Isaac, and Jacob, and of the prophets. Yet because of the influence of Marcion, and possibly also the opposition of the Jews to the Christian faith, the Old Testament has been given a relatively unimportant place in the life of the church. Thus, for example, almost all the texts traditionally read in the service in churches that follow the liturgical church year are taken from the New Testament.

Marcion, who did not understand the spirit of the Old Testament, failed to see its connection with the New Testament, which he proposed to cut off entirely from the religion of the Old. His intention was to exalt Jesus and the New Testament message. The church has been at one with Marcion in emphasizing the uniqueness of Jesus and the decisive character of his work. It has not been satisfied to regard only the person of Jesus as unique, but has sometimes even tried to show that his teaching and ministry were entirely new. Many have endeavored to show that the sayings of Jesus were completely original, and that his conception of the kingdom and of God as Father was unique with him. They have

89

resented any attempt to show that parallels to his teaching could be found in the Old Testament and in other sources. The church has concentrated on the New Testament and often insisted that its message is unique even in relationship to the Old Testament. The result has been that the Old Testament has been reduced to a status of preparation and prediction. God was of course active in the Old Testament, too, but his activity was merely preparatory for the real redemption that was to come in Christ. His actions before Christ were thought of in terms of preparation for the future, not as events redemptive in themselves. It was assumed that the prophets were not speaking of contemporary events but of the future act of God in Christ. Even if it was admitted that they spoke of the events of their own time, it was held that the real, deeper meaning of their words had reference to the future rather than to the contemporary situation.

Yet there has also been the conception of a continuous action on God's part and a progressive revelation of his purpose from the beginning to the end. The Old Testament promise becomes clearer and more universal as time goes on, and finds its fulfillment in the command of Jesus to "make disciples of all nations." From that point on the development continues until the final consummation. While the church emphasized the event of Christ in its message of the New Testament, it was also recognized that God had not yet finished his work, and that it would not be finished until he made "a new heaven and a new earth." This conception might be presented graphically as a straight line extending from creation to the consummation.

Just as the Old Testament was preparatory to the coming of Christ, so the mission of the church in its preaching of the gospel in all the world is a preparation for the return of Christ and the establishment of the eternal kingdom. It is this which has been the traditional conception of the biblical perspective.

In the contemporary interpretations of the New Testament, the tendency seems to be to emphasize the event of Christ as the central act of redemption which dominates both the past and the future. The death and resurrection of Jesus is *the* redemptive event in which all of God's activity is concentrated. This type of interpretation is seen in the doctrine of the old and the new age, which we have already discussed,[1] in the conception of the event of Christ as the mid-point in history, and in the emphasis on "realized eschatology."

Oscar Cullman makes the concept of biblical time the decisive factor in his interpretation of the New Testament. In contrast to the Greek conception of time as recurrent ages or cycles which are indefinitely repeated, the biblical conception of time is a straight and ascending line. "Salvation is bound to a *continuous time process* which embraces past, present and future. Revelation and salvation take place along the course of an ascending time line. . . . All points of this redemptive line are related to the *one historical fact* at the mid-point, a fact which precisely in its unrepeatable character, which marks all historical events, is decisive for salvation. This fact is the death and resurrection of Jesus Christ."[2] The events which transpired in the first century of the Christian era, the time of the coming of Christ, are the center of time, the mid-point of the line. His coming creates a new division of time, because it ushers in the new age, although the final period beginning with the Parousia has not yet come. In contrast to Judaism, the New Testament holds that the decisive event is not in the future but has already taken place with the coming of Christ, in whose lifetime the king-

---

[1] See pp. 51-52.
[2] Oscar Cullmann, *Christ and Time,* trans. Floyd V. Filson (Philadelphia, 1950), pp. 32-33.

dom of God impinges upon men. Although Jesus simultaneously
holds fast "to the future character of this Kingdom, . . . he sees
Satan already fallen from heaven."[3]

To illustrate his thesis, Cullman uses a figure which has become
very popular. "The decisive battle in a war may already have occurred in a relatively early stage of the war, and yet the war still
continues . . . the decisive effect of that battle . . . already means
victory. But the war must still be carried on for an indefinite time,
until 'Victory Day.' "[4] Just so the Cross and the Resurrection were
the decisive battle, and it is already concluded; yet the conflict remains and the war continues. Christ rules now, but he encounters
opposition. The time of the church since Pentecost is the reign of
Christ, *regnum Christi,* which is anterior and preparatory to the
reign of God (I Cor. 15:24-28; Phil. 2:9-11; Phil. 3:20-21).[5]
The new man in Christ belongs to the *eschaton.* In Christ the new
creation has taken place, and the church is the fulfillment of the
promised people of God in "the last time."

Cullmann's emphasis on the decisive character of the mid-point
does not mean that he does not hold to a future part of the time
line and to a new event that is to come. Even though the decisive
battle has been won at the mid-point, "D Day," the "Victory Day"
is still in the future. Victory Day is the new event, when "the Holy
Spirit, the *pneuma,* lays hold of the entire world of the flesh *(sarx),*
of matter."[6] Up to that time "the Holy Spirit penetrates into the
world of the body only temporarily," but at that time the penetra-
tion will become complete, just as at the Resurrection Christ's body
became a spiritual body. This future event is also decisive, because
it is then that sin and death will be destroyed and the world re-
created.[7] Then "he who raised Christ Jesus from the dead will give
life to your mortal bodies also through his Spirit which dwells in

[3]*Ibid.,* pp. 82-83.
[4]*Ibid.,* p. 84.
[5]*Ibid.,* pp. 151 ff., 185 ff. Cf. Cullmann's *The Early Church,* trans. A. J. B.
Higgins (Philadelphia, 1956), pp. 105 ff.
[6]*Christ and Time,* p. 141.
[7]*The Early Church,* p. 147.

you" (Rom. 8:11). This hope rests on the resurrection of Jesus, for in the Resurrection the Spirit did receive dominion over the body already within history at the middle of the time line. Victory Day is therefore dependent on the event at the mid-point, D Day, and would be absolutely impossible without it.[8] Thus Cullmann returns to the idea of the mid-point, making it determinative for what happens in the future.

The conception of "realized eschatology," advocated especially by C. H. Dodd, is somewhat analogous to the views of Cullmann, but without the emphasis on the concept of time or the victory in the future. Jesus and the New Testament writers proclaim that the kingdom of God *has* come. There are several passages in the Gospels which become key words in the argument: "But if it is by the finger of God that I cast out demons, then the kingdom of God has come upon you" (Luke 11:20). "The time is fulfilled, and the kingdom of God is at hand" (Mark 1:15); "the kingdom of God has come near" (Luke 10:11). The perfect tense of the Greek, "has come," in these passages denotes an action which has already taken place but whose effect continues into the present. The kingdom has come and is now here. In contrast to the Old Testament, according to Dodd, the New Testament declares "that the expected event has actually taken place. In the coming of Jesus Christ, His death and resurrection, the prophecies have been fulfilled and the kingdom of God is revealed." His death and resurrection "are eschatological events in the full sense; that is to say, they are not simply important events, not even the most important events in a series, but unique and final events, in which the God beyond history intervened conclusively to reveal His kingdom on earth."[9] The early disciples held that the eschatological process had already begun in the death and resurrection of Jesus. They thought of the event of Christ as final, but when his return did not come immediately, certain readjustments of their outlook had to be made. The church began to reconstruct the traditional scheme of Jewish eschatology,

---

[8] *Christ and Time*, pp. 142-143.
[9] Dodd, *History and the Gospel* (New York, 1938), p. 35.

94 GOD WHO REDEEMS

which had been broken up by the declaration that the kingdom of God had already come. Thus the traditional eschatological scheme returned and found its climax in Revelation. This development led into a blind alley: "In the second century its stream ran out into the barren sands of millenarianism, which in the end was disavowed by the church."[10] The church then returned to the original emphasis on the fact that the kingdom of God has come. "Whereas Jewish eschatology looked to the close of the historical process as the necessary fulfillment upon which the meaning of history depends, Christianity found the fulfillment of history in an actual series of events within history—namely the life, death and resurrection of Jesus Christ, and the emergence of the Church as the bearer of His Spirit. History, indeed, still goes on, and at long last it will have an ending. But meanwhile, the true *eschaton,* the event in which its meaning is conclusively revealed, has become an object of experience."[11] "The Kingdom of God is not something yet to come. It has come with Jesus Christ, and its coming was perceived to be eternal in its quality. That eternal quality is manifested in time by the continuous life of the Church, centered in the sacrament in which the crisis of the death and resurrection of Christ is perpetually present."[12]

In Dodd's view, although there is, of course, a future event for the church, since history continues and the church still lives in the world, this future event has lost much of its significance. It is not really a new event, nor will it bring anything new. "There will be an end when the Church, or redeemed humanity, has grown into the stature of the fulness of Christ. But there will be nothing in the End which is not already given explicitly to the Church. Christ has already conquered the powers of evil, and in Him men already have access to the glorious and immortal life of the eternal order."[13]

---

[10]Dodd, *The Apostolic Preaching and its Development* (New York, 1960), p. 41.

[11]Dodd, in *The Kingdom of God and History* ("Official Oxford Conference Books," Vol. III [Chicago, 1938]), pp. 23-24.

[12]*Ibid.,* p. 35.

[13]*Ibid.,* p. 28.

The *eschaton* has come, the victory has been won, and the kingdom
of God is here. The same thought is expressed clearly by G. H. C.
MacGregor: "Whereas contemporary Judaism looked for the ultimate defeat of the evil powers only at the last day, so that to that
extent the world was at present inaccessible to divine succour, Paul
looked back to that defeat as having been already accomplished by
God in Christ through the Cross. There the powers had been defeated once and for all in what can only be thought of as an act of
cosmic redemption."[14]

What could be the ultimate conclusion of this type of interpretation of the New Testament is drawn by a Swedish theologian,
Torgny Bohlin. Under the influence of Cullmann and especially
of Dodd, Bohlin maintains that the event of Christ is the center of
history, the mid-point, from which light is thrown on the past (creation) and on the future *(eschaton)*. All time is concentrated in
Christ's victory as man on earth. "In biblical thought eternity
means a divine concentration of all time in a single point, i.e., in
Christ as the mid-point."[15] Eternity lies at the middle of time,
not at the end. The decisive event has already taken place, although the Christian does not know its full meaning as yet. The
Cross is the turning point in history where all times meet, and
where the lordship of Christ over all time is revealed, so that the
rule of Christ in the present is henceforth the decisive factor.[16]
While Cullmann speaks of a future event that will mean the transformation of the flesh into the spiritual body, Bohlin insists that
the end has only a retrospective significance. Everything has happened already at the mid-point, and the Christian has been given
the new life and lives in the new age. He is not looking for salvation, but has it. To be sure, he does not as yet realize the greatness
of the victory which happened on the Cross, nor the full glory of
the life that he now lives in the flesh. This will become clear to him

[14]G. H. C. MacGregor, "Principalities and Powers: The Cosmic Background
of Paul's Thought," *New Testament Studies*, I, No. 1 (1954), 28.

[15]Torgny Bohlin, *Den korsfäste Skaparen* (Uppsala, 1952), p. 3.

[16]*Ibid.*, p. 35.

on the last day. The final event is not an active event, and nothing
will really happen except a fuller realization of what has already
taken place at the mid-point. The terms used to describe this future event are cognitive: to attain to inner clarity, to realize, perceive, know, understand. Then it will become clear that the Christian already *in this life had* all the blessings which Christ had secured for him. "The fulfillment in the eschatological future simply
means that the Christian at the final point of the temporal development realizes the totality of the riches in what happened at the
mid-point of history where all time is concentrated, i.e., that the
thought of Christ as Savior and Redeemer becomes a living reality."[17] The eschatological future does not bring anything new in
addition to what the Christian already has, but he will then realize
and perceive what he already had in this life. He will then have
full knowledge and personal experience of what his life means.

This emphasis on "realized eschatology" does indeed elucidate
one important aspect of New Testament thought—the uniqueness
of the event of Christ and the reality of the new creation of life in
him. In our analysis of the biblical events we have pointed out that
each succeeding event is greater in certain respects than the previous ones, even though as acts of God they are of the same nature
and are a part of his eternal purpose. The New Testament can
therefore speak in absolute terms of the victory that Christ has won
and the redemption that he has secured. The same absolute statements can be made about the new life in Christ. The Christian
knows himself as redeemed from the powers of sin, death, and the
devil, and he can say confidently with John, "we are God's children
*now."* But in spite of this emphasis on the present the New Testament looks forward to a new act of God, to a fulfillment, a consummation, which will transform this age into the age to come.
This look toward the future is by no means confined to the apocalyptic passages in the New Testament; it is found everywhere. It
represents the conviction that what God has begun he will finish

---

[17]*Ibid.*, p. 406.

"at the day of Jesus Christ," a phrase from one of Paul's letters, Phil.
1:6. It is noteworthy that not even Bohlin can escape speaking
about the future, since history goes on, the church exists in the
world, and the Christian continues to "live in the flesh." In order
to put all the emphasis on the mid-point it would be necessary to
concentrate on some special passages of the New Testament material and to ignore a great deal of the rest.

"Realized eschatology" tends to ignore the Old Testament. In
almost all of the works just cited, references to the Old Testament
are limited to what is predictive of the day of the Lord and the
last days. In the process of contrasting the "realized eschatology" of
the New Testament and "Jewish eschatology," the eschatology of
the prophets is not dealt with. The logic of "Jewish eschatology" is
stated by Dodd in the following terms. Through the Exodus out of
Egypt God had created for himself a people who were to be a people of kings and priests, a people for his own possession. But their
own history seemed to deny this claim, since the people forsook
Yahweh for idols and thus ended up in captivity. History seemed
to deny the election. But this denial will be turned into affirmation
when in the future God acts finally and reveals the people of the
saints of the Most High in the glory of the age to come. This is
the vision of seers and prophets, but it is a vision and not historical
fact. "The vision is indeed a vision of an event . . . . but it can after
all be described only in fantastic and mythological terms, since it
belongs to the unrealized future."[18]

When we examine more closely the text of the Old Testament,
however, we realize that this does not do justice to the prophets
and their message. In the first place, it makes them speak only of
the future and in fanciful and extravagant terms. Actually, as we
have seen in the analysis of the Old Testament events, the prophets
speak much of the past acts of God, and call the people back to
trust in Yahweh and to faithfulness to the covenant. The events
which they interpreted were redemptive acts of God through

---

[18]Dodd, in *Kingdom of God and History*, p. 22.

which Yahweh carried out his purpose for his people and humanity. Even the prophets of the Old Testament could say that God had already come, for it was he who had come to Abraham, to the slaves in Egypt and to the exiles in Babylon. He had come to them with redemption and life. Thus the prophet looks back to the past for his message to the people in the present. God had established them as his people through his redemptive acts, and he is the faithful God of the covenant and of steadfast love.

Furthermore, the prophet speaks of the present and the immediate future. The Exodus was God's redemptive act which would bring Israel to the promised land. Isaiah did not address himself to some distant future, but to his own contemporaries, Ahaz and his people. He called upon them to trust in Yahweh in order that they might be established and remain as a people. The prophets of the Exile saw in the return a manifestation in their own time of the same redemptive power God had manifested in the Exodus: they saw an event through which he would now create a new people and a new age. They were not speaking of a covenant to be established five hundred years later in the New Testament, but of a present covenant which God would establish with the returning exiles. This aspect of the prophetic voice is completely ignored in the analysis made by Dodd, who describes the later apocalyptic development and ascribes it to the Old Testament prophets as a whole. The later development was indeed "Jewish eschatology," which Dodd says was taken over by the church and modified. The New Testament proclamation is really much more parallel to the prophetic eschatology, for it is the act of God in Christ that the New Testament people proclaim and on the basis of which they look for a future redemption.

Dodd's interpretation also fails to take the New Testament in its wholeness seriously. Thessalonians, chapter 13 of Mark, and Revelation are dismissed as "Jewish eschatology" which runs out in the barren sands of millenarianism and is repudiated by the church. The hope for a future realization of the present experience of salvation is not confined to these passages, however; it is embedded in the very center of the New Testament. It is only by an arbitrary application of the "demythologizing" principle that this element can be eliminated. The Synoptic Gospels, Paul, Hebrews, and even John look forward to a final event which will complete and fulfill the redemption promised in Christ. If we think of the biblical perspective in terms of God's purpose, the goal is still in the future. God has not finished his work. There remains a promise of a future event, "a sabbath rest for the people of God." What this event will be we may not know very well, but it will be in character with what God has already revealed of himself and his purpose in Jesus Christ.

Finally, "realized eschatology" fails to take into account the experience of the Christians through the centuries: the continuous struggle with evil forces. It leaves the problem of evil unsolved, as though the powers of evil have been reduced to inconsequence in the course of history since the triumph of Christ. It does not take seriously the abiding power of sin, death, and the devil. In this scheme, such conceptions as evil powers and a real devil may be dismissed as mythological fancies that we need no longer take seriously, but the New Testament speaks realistically of the powers of evil. Jesus warned his disciples that there would be enemies who would persecute and even kill them. He warned, too, that in the face of opposition they might be tempted to turn away from following him. He taught them to pray: "Lead us not into temptation, but deliver us from evil." In the same letter which extolls the Christian experience of being new creatures in Christ, chosen in him "before the foundation of the world," and in which the church is spoken of as the body of Christ, we also have passages which urge the Christians to "Put on the whole armor of God, that you may be able to stand against the wiles of the devil. . . . take the whole armor of God, that you may be able to withstand in the evil day, and having done all, to stand" (Eph. 6:11-13). Evidently some of the New Testament writers do not know about the defeat of the devil as an accomplished fact. "Your adversary the devil prowls around like a roaring lion, seeking some one to devour. Resist him" (I Pet. 5:8-9). "Let any one who thinks that he stands take heed lest he fall" (I Cor. 10:12). This realistic outlook describes the Christian life now after the resurrection of Christ. The enemies are powerful and the Christian stands in jeopardy every hour. Therefore Jesus says: "Watch and pray that you may not enter into temptation."

Realistic recognition of the continuing power of evil stands side by side in the New Testament with a confident assurance that these evil powers are not really able to hurt the believer who is in Christ. When Jesus tells his disciples of the persecutions and sufferings they will have to endure, he says, "Some of you they will put to death . . . but not a hair of your head will perish" (Luke 21:16-18). Justin Martyr is said to have told his judges: "You can kill us, but you cannot hurt us." Paradoxically, the New Testament recognizes freely the terrible power of the evil forces arrayed against the people of God, but at the same time proclaims confidently that the Lord is able to keep his own. The Old Testament psalmist spoke the same language. "The Lord is my light and my salvation; whom shall I fear? The Lord is the stronghold of my life; of whom shall I be afraid?" (Ps. 27:1).

The power of evil is not only without, in heavenly places and in the world; it is also within the Christian himself. To use a phrase that became current later, in the Lutheran tradition, the Christian is *simul iustus et peccator,* at once righteous and a sinner. His struggle is not only against the devil and the world, but also against "the flesh." Paul found that his converts failed to live up to the standard of the new life in Christ. The Corinthians were engaged in such bitter quarrels that even in the celebration of the Lord's Supper they denied the unity of the body of Christ. The Galatians were ready to forsake Paul and adopt a gospel that was not a gospel. Even the Twelve quarrelled and had to be rebuked by Jesus. It is possible that because of their great experience of the grace of God the early Christians were more confident of the victory over sin and of their own ability to live the new life in Christ than were those who followed later in the history of the church. The doctrine *simul iustus et peccator* possibly represents a pessimism based on the evident failure of the church and the Christians to "walk by the Spirit."[19] The very fact that Paul had occasion to urge his converts to "put off the old nature" indicates not only that they ought to do so, but also that they needed to do so. Here again the New Testament recognizes the continuous struggle in which the Christian is engaged, and here, too, the recognition of the power of "the flesh" stands side by side with the confidence in the victory of the Spirit. The disciple has to walk a narrow and difficult way, and he must therefore "walk by the Spirit" so as not to "gratify the desires of the flesh."

In view of the New Testament emphasis on the continuing struggle against the old man, the flesh, and the devil, and considering that even the earliest Christians experienced the abiding might of the powers of evil, it seems unrealistic and irrevelant to us to speak of the great victory that has taken place on D Day or at the mid-point. Thus we find Cullmann's analogy and time-scheme deceiving. The final and decisive battle to which the whole Bible looks forward comes at the end, when the kingdom of God shall be established and all opposition to his will shall be eliminated. Paul knew very well that he had not arrived, but that he was on the way to the goal which God himself had set for him. (Rom. 8:22-23; Phil. 3:12-14).

If we take the time line seriously as a guide to our understanding of God's acts in history, we should regard the event of Christ as one event in the long series of events recorded in the Bible and interpreted in terms of judgment, redemption, and promise. Its uniqueness is not to be found in separating it from the Old Testament. The New Testament insists that it is an act of the same God who created the world and still holds it in his hand. This new act of God is of the same nature, character, and purpose as the redemptive acts of God in the past, but it carries God's purpose further and reveals more clearly his redemptive concern for the world. It also

---

[19]Cf. Paul Althaus, *Paulus und Luther über den Menschen* (Gütersloh, 1938), pp. 46 ff.

102 — GOD WHO REDEEMS

presupposes the completion of his purpose in the future, by an event complementary to it, the final triumph of God.

As we see it, the uniqueness of the event of Christ lies primarily in the person of Jesus. In the Old Testament God used persons whom he called out of humanity to become the instruments of his purpose and the bearers of his revelation. Because God called and equipped them, human beings could become his agents in the redemptive process. Jesus, on the other hand, is the *Son* who comes into the world to participate in the struggle as a man among men. The Old Testament was indeed preparatory for this coming of the Son of God, in the sense that each event is a preparation for the next and marks an advance along the time line of God's purpose, but in the same sense, the event of Christ also becomes a part of the time line, an episode in the continuous, redemptive activity of God, and a preparation for a new event which is inherent in the promise of complete redemption and final victory.

## THE INCARNATION

The New Testament insists that Jesus came from above, from God, into this world. In the past God had used men to be the bearers of his revelation, but now the Son of God himself became man and lived on this earth as man among men. There is a clear line of demarcation between the divine and the human; if it were asked whether Jesus as a man approached that line from below, from a human origin, and perhaps crossed it and *became* thus the divine Son of God, or whether he crossed that line from above and became man, the answer of the New Testament is unequivocal. Jesus came from above into the world. He did not *become* the Son of God, he *was* the Son of God. This is the universal confession of the church on the basis of the New Testament.

This conviction as to the person of Jesus is expressed in the New Testament in various ways. There are a number of passages in which it is said that he was *sent* into the world. In the parable of the wicked husbandmen the owner of the vineyard sends a number of his servants to his workers, and when they fail to effect a settlement, he finally sends his only son in the hope that "they will respect my son" (Matt. 21:33 ff.). "For God sent the Son into the world, not to condemn the world, but that the world might be saved through him" (John 3:17). "But when the time had fully come, God sent forth his Son" (Gal. 4:4). The passages in which Jesus is spoken of as the agent through whom God has created and sustains the world clearly indicate that he existed in the form of God and came into the world (John 1:1-3; Col. 1:16-17; Heb. 1:2-3). The God of creation and the God of redemption are one and the same God, and the Son is the agent through whom God carries out his work. Paul declares that "though he was in the form of God, [he] did not count equality with God a thing to be grasped, but emptied himself, taking the form of a servant, being born in the likeness of men" (Phil. 2:6-7). This conviction that Jesus came into the world from God, that he was sent by God, and that he was God, is expressed clearly in the New Testament. The work he performs is God's work, whether in creation, in redemption, or in the final consummation. Accordingly, his birth of Mary would not have been his beginning as the Son of God, but only as the Incarnation of the Son of God.

There is much less in the New Testament that seeks to suggest *how* he came into the world. The church has confessed through the ages that he was "conceived by the Holy Spirit, born of the virgin Mary," but the passages that can be quoted in support of this doctrine are very few indeed. That he was "descended from David according to the flesh" (Rom. 1:3) has by some been taken to imply the virgin birth. The same has been asserted of the passage, Gal. 4:4, "born of woman." Both of these passages simply refer to his human birth. Paul's summary of the gospel message in I Cor. 15:1-4, which represents the tradition he had received and transmitted, contains no allusion to this doctrine. Paul bears witness to the reality of Jesus' human birth, but he has no statement which even alludes to the manner of the Incarnation. His chief christological passage (Phil. 2:5 ff.) says simply that "he was in the form of God" and he was "born in the likeness of men." In John 1:13

a variant reading has *qui natus est*, singular, which would refer to the Logos rather than to "the children of God." There is no ancient Greek manuscript authority for this reading, although it is quoted by some of the later church fathers. Since John speaks freely, in his first letter, of the Christians as being born of God, it is natural to follow the manuscript tradition here and understand this saying as referring to the Christians as "born of God."

The witness to the doctrine of the virgin birth is limited in the New Testament to the two Gospels, Matthew and Luke, which contain an account of the birth of Jesus.

In the story of the annunciation to Mary in Luke 1:26 ff. we have an account which is highly influenced by Old Testament ideas. The angel greeted the maiden with the words: "Hail, O favored one, the Lord is with you!" What would a Hebrew maiden in Galilee in the reign of Herod the Great understand by such a greeting? The highest favor that God could bestow upon a Hebrew woman would be to become the mother of the Messiah. It is not at all strange that Mary became troubled and "considered in her mind what sort of greeting this might be." Then the angel spoke more plainly and declared: "You will conceive in your womb and bear a son." The description of the child that is to be born is given in the traditional terms of the Messiah. "He will be great, and will be called the Son of the Most High; and the Lord God will give to him the throne of his father David, and he will reign over the house of Jacob for ever; and of his kingdom there will be no end" (Luke 1:32-33). Nothing in these words goes beyond the traditional picture of the Messiah as a king who will inherit the throne of David and rule in Israel forever. When Mary was still troubled, the angel assured her: "The Holy Spirit will come upon you, and the power of the Most High will overshadow you; therefore the child to be born will be called holy, the Son of God" (Luke 1:35). In the Hebrew, the name of God here is the ancient *El-Elyon*, "the God Most High." The title Son of God was often applied to the kings of Israel and especially to the future king, the Messiah. The promise to Mary was that by the power of God she would become the mother of the Messiah.[20] Nothing in this account conclusively points to the virgin birth except the cryptic statement by Mary, "How can this be, since I have no husband?" Since it had just been said that Mary was "betrothed to a man whose name was Joseph," and the conception was to take place in the future, there is no satisfactory explanation of this strange statement.

The only other passage in Luke's Gospel that suggests the virgin birth is the parenthetical statement, "as was supposed," in Luke 3:23. It is really remarkable that in this whole section of the infancy stories there is nothing explicit that goes beyond the traditional Jewish expectation of a king Messiah. There is no hint of suffering and death, and no allusion to the Resurrection, as might have been expected in a tradition that grew up and was formulated in the church after these events had taken place. The child to be born would be a son of David, and he would fulfill the promises made "to Abraham and to his posterity for ever" (Luke 1:55). If the doctrine of the virgin birth is to be found in this Lucan account, it is by inference rather than in explicit statements. If we did not have the account in Matthew, it is doubtful that we could have derived the doctrine of the virgin birth from this account in Luke.

We rely solely, therefore, upon the single, unequivocal statement of this doctrine in Matt. 1:18: "When his mother Mary had been betrothed to Joseph, before they came together she was found to be with child of the Holy Spirit." The Incarnation is explained as an activity of the Holy Spirit. The New Testament thus gives unquestionable authority for the doctrine of the virgin birth. There is a strong emphasis on the activity of the Spirit in these birth narratives that reminds us of the first creation in Genesis, when "the

---

[20]The Swedish theologian Harald Sahlin comes to the same conclusion in an article entitled, "*Några reflexioner kring sensus obvius vid tolkningen av Bibeln,*" in *Svensk Teologisk Kvartalskrift,* 1960, pp. 246 ff. Sahlin argues that when Mary says "I have no husband" she speaks for "the Daughter of Zion" (Isa. 62:11) — that is, Zion, the people of God — who is "Forsaken" (Isa. 62:4). To Zion now comes the Messiah who will "reign over the house of Jacob for ever" (Luke 1:33). We may add that the Magnificat likewise expresses the triumphant confidence that the promises "to Abraham and to his posterity for ever" are now being fulfilled.

Spirit of God was moving over the face of the waters." Now the power of the Spirit of God is manifested again in the new creation as the Son of God comes into the world. The promise to Mary is for the presence of the Holy Spirit. Jesus is guided by the Holy Spirit in his baptism and temptation, and he announces at the beginning of his ministry: "The Spirit of the Lord is upon me." That which is now taking place is the manifestation of the Spirit and power of God. This emphasis is found in Matthew's account. Although Matthew takes it for granted that Jesus was born to a virgin mother, as the Greek version of the prophecy to which he alludes has it, the important point in his story of the birth of Jesus is not the manner of the child's conception but the fulfillment of the prophecy "Emmanuel, God with us." Just as the prophet had attempted by the sign of the birth of the child to convince Ahaz that God was with him (Isaiah, chapter 7), so now the evangelist attempts to show that the prophecy "God is with us"—is favorably inclined toward us—is fulfilled in the birth of the child in Bethlehem. Matthew's Gospel, which begins with the prophecy "God with us," ends with the promise "Lo, I am with you always, to the close of the age."

John's Gospel begins with the eternal Logos, and then simply announces that "the Word became flesh," i.e., a human being. The contrast between verse one and verse fourteen is emphatic and deliberate. He who was in the beginning, became; he who was with God, dwelt among us; he who was God, became man. This is the New Testament confession of the great mystery. The reality of the Incarnation is affirmed or implied in most of the New Testament. Jesus was God's only Son, he stood in a special relationship to his heavenly Father, and he came from above into the world. The New Testament does not seem to have been particularly concerned to ask *how* the Incarnation took place, or *how* he came. If this had been a matter of real concern to the early church, there would have been more evidence of it in the New Testament writers. They were content to affirm that he was God's only Son and that he came into the world from God. Inevitably, as time passed the question was raised how this event occurred. Those who asked could find some guidance in the tradition recorded in Matthew and Luke, but these accounts do not explain the mystery of the birth of God's son as a man among men. The much later doctrine of the Immaculate Conception of the Virgin Mary is an attempt to deal with what the doctrine of the virgin birth left unresolved, how the holy God could be born of sinful man. We can see in it the desire of the church to separate the person of Jesus from sinful humanity, in order to show that in his person there is a new start and a new creation. Yet such a method is alien to the New Testament and a somewhat ironical development, since the New Testament insists that Jesus was identified with sinful humanity in order to bear and atone for its sin. He shared the lot of the men among whom he moved, and was "not ashamed to call them brethren" (Heb. 2:11). No amount of speculation will help us to solve the mystery of his coming, nor will it improve on the simplicity of the ancient confession: ". . . conceived by the Holy Spirit, born of the Virgin Mary." We cannot pierce the mystery that John expresses in the words: "and the Word became flesh."

## THE PERSON OF CHRIST

The church in its ancient confession has stated that Jesus is true God and true man. This means that the Incarnation was real. It was not simply a theophany, as the ancient Docetists claimed. He not only *appeared* as a man, he *became* and *was* man. The Gospel record is quite factual about this. Luke declares that he increased like any other human being "in wisdom and in stature, and in favor with God and man" (Luke 2:52). He was hungry, weary, perplexed, tempted, in need of comfort, like other men. "Since therefore the children share in flesh and blood, he himself likewise partook of the same nature" (Heb. 2:14).

That the Incarnation was real implies that Jesus accepted the limitations under which human life is lived in this world: physical, mental, and spiritual limitations.

We usually have no difficulty in believing that during his earthly

ministry Jesus was subject to the same physical limitations and necessities that we are. He had to eat, drink, and sleep like other men.
He was confined in time and space. If he was in Jerusalem and
wanted to go to Galilee, he had to walk just like his disciples. None
of the marvelous feats of transportation are reported of him that
we find in the later apocryphal acts of the apostles. He walked and
he got tired. Also, if he was in one place, he could not be in another
place at the same time; if he was in Capernaum, he could not be
in Jerusalem. The physical limitations of time and space applied
to him as to all men.

It is a little more difficult for the believer to accept the fact that
human limitations applied also to Jesus' mind. A human being
does not know the future, nor can he know what is happening elsewhere. It is, of course, claimed that certain extra-sensory experiences
transcend these limitations, but they are as yet fairly unknown and
mysterious. A being to whom the future and the past were the
same as the present, and who knew what was happening everywhere, would not be a true human being. The humanity of such
a person would be at best unreal.

Some passages in the Gospels indicate that Jesus did not know
all things. At the feeding of the five thousand he asked his disciples,
"How many loaves have you? Go and see." (Mark 6:38). At the
meeting with Martha he asked where they had laid Lazarus. He
also stated that not even the Son knew when the last day would
come (Matt. 24:36). To interpret these passages in such a way
that no limitation on his knowledge is implied would be to read a
theory into the record. If we take his humanity seriously, we must
grant that as a human being he had to depend upon the human
ways of acquiring knowledge, just as Luke suggests.

Since he was truly human, he would also have had to walk by
faith in dependence on God step by step on the way of life. He
would have had to accept the limitation of the spirit as well as of
mind. Here the record is quite clear. Jesus lived in utter dependence on the heavenly Father. He found it necessary, especially at
times of crisis in his ministry, to spend extended time in prayer and

meditation. Several times, it is recorded, he spent a night in lonely vigil and in prayer to God. John's Gospel, which strongly emphasizes his status as the divine Son of God, is at the same time most emphatic in asserting his complete dependence on the Father in his own words. "The Son can do nothing of his own accord" (John 5:19). "I can do nothing on my own authority" (5:30). "I have come down from heaven, not to do my own will, but the will of him who sent me" (6:38). "My teaching is not mine, but his who sent me" (7:16). The works that he does have been given to him by the Father (5:36). He does nothing on the suggestion of anybody else, whether his mother (2:3), his brethren (7:3), or the sisters of Lazarus (11:3), but when "his hour has come," the hour set by the Father, he goes in perfect obedience.

It is indeed extremely precarious for us to try to analyze the personal development of Jesus and the psychological processes of his mind, for the Gospels do not provide enough information to enable us to know "the inner life of Jesus," but the structure of the Synoptic Gospels indicates that he came gradually to a realization of his call as God's agent in redemption. The great excitement created by the preaching of John the Baptist became a call to Jesus to begin his own ministry. The baptism of Jesus marked his definite call to his own particular mission. At that moment, he became assured that he was God's anointed Servant, called to be the fulfillment of the promises made to the fathers. That he had meditated on this before, during his years in Nazareth, is rather likely, but his baptism became, as it were, the installation into the messianic office. "He saw the heavens opened and the Spirit descending upon him like a dove; and a voice came from heaven, 'Thou art my beloved Son; with thee I am well pleased'" (Mark 1:10-11).

The experience of the call did not solve the problem of how his ministry was to be carried out. We can possibly understand the three temptations as suggesting different ways in which the messianic task might be carried out. There were many traditions in Judaism about what would happen when the Messiah appeared. The messianic age would be an age of plenty. The food supply, which was always short, would then be abundant. The devil suggested, "Give them bread, that is what they expect," and Jesus answered that hunger is not removed by bread alone. Another expectation was that the Messiah would appear suddenly in the temple at a great festival like the Passover and be received by all the people. Or, he would come as a great warrior at the head of an army and capture all the kingdoms of the world. These were some of the conceptions of the character and mission of the Messiah. Jesus rejected all these. Then in the visit to Nazareth, according to Luke, he announced his own program in the words of the great prophecy of Isaiah: "The Spirit of the Lord is upon me, because he has anointed me to preach good news to the poor. He has sent me to proclaim release to the captives and recovering of sight to the blind, to set at liberty those who are oppressed, to proclaim the acceptable year of the Lord" (Luke 4:18-19). This was to be the character of his ministry and the way of his life. This passage from Isaiah stands in Luke's Gospel as a text that is developed and illustrated in the subsequent narratives.

. As time went on, it became more and more clear that the people would not accept his message. The shadow of the Cross began to fall over his way. He began to announce this to the disciples and to prepare them for the catastrophe. The Gospel records have him say that he was to be arrested, crucified, and on the third day rise again.

Did he know what was going to happen, the way we assume that God knows what is going to happen? If he did, he was not after all a true human being. If he knew as God what he could not know as man, the unity of his personality is destroyed. The answer would seem to lie in the fact that he lived by faith as a human being day by day. There is a clear distinction between knowledge and faith, although these terms are closely related. His confidence in the Resurrection after three days, i.e., after a short time, was a confession of faith in his heavenly Father. In a sense it was the same faith as that of the prophets who declared, "God is with us" and "The God of Jacob is our refuge." Thus a Christian may say: "I know that my Redeemer lives, and that I shall live also," using "know" to express a conviction and a confidence based on faith. Jesus believed himself to be called of God to be the Messiah, the promised Redeemer, the Fulfiller of the promises of God. Although he saw that the way he must go led to apparent defeat, to rejection, crucifixion, and death, he believed that his heavenly Father had called him, that he must go this way in obedience to his will, and that the Father would raise him up victorious over death. This was his faith. He staked his life on the reality of this call, and it was true. He lived a truly human life in faith, trust, and obedience.

As a true human being, he had to be like us in all things except in one, and that an important respect. It is declared in the New Testament that Jesus was without sin. He lived in perfect obedience to his heavenly Father. "He committed no sin; no guile was found on his lips" (I Pet. 2:22). "For our sake he made him to be sin who knew no sin, so that in him we might become the righteousness of God" (II Cor. 5:21). He is "one who in every respect has been tempted as we are, yet without sinning" (Heb. 4:15). Our humanity, therefore, is not the measure of his humanity; rather, it is in comparison with him that we find how far short we are of being the true human beings that God intended us to be. Our humanity is a sinful, fallen humanity, darkened in understanding, perverted in will, and wretched in feeling. In him there was no disobedience, to separate him from his heavenly Father. He could say: "He who sent me is with me; he has not left me alone, for I always do what is pleasing to him" (John 8:29). He stood in an unbroken relationship to his heavenly Father, and God had not given the Spirit by measure to him (cf. John 3:34).

If this was true about him, the possibilities open to him were beyond anything that we can understand and measure by our distorted experience of the human existence. God could work in him freely and powerfully without opposition from a perverted will. What he did was God's work. Both Jesus and the New Testament writers attribute his work to God. "If it is by the finger of God that I cast out demons, then the kingdom of God has come upon you" (Luke 11:20). "God was in Christ reconciling the world to himself." In him there were no obstacles or barriers to the grace and power of God. He was a true human being, living in utter dependence on God, subject to his will, and ready at all times to go the way the Father had determined.

This view of the humanity of Jesus is suggested by Paul in the christological passage in Phil. 2:5 ff. He was in the form of God, but "he emptied himself, taking the form of a servant, being born in the likeness of men" (Phil. 2:7). The self-emptying, kenosis doctrine derived from this passage has had a long and ambiguous history. It is probably true that anyone who tries to think of the Incarnation at all must arrive at some conception of kenosis. The Son of God did not appear here on earth in "the glory which [he] had with [the Father] before the world was made" (John 17:5). The Gospels tell the story of a man who grew up in Nazareth, carried on his ministry in Galilee and Jerusalem, and was "crucified under Pontius Pilate." He must have "emptied himself," laid aside his divine attributes, in order to live here on earth as a man. Many questions and objections may be raised against this doctrine of kenosis.[21] How could the Son of God temporarily surrender the government of the universe in order to appear on earth as a man? Does it not imply that he ceased for a time to be God and became man, then resumed his position as God again? Does it not mean that on resuming his divinity he ceased again to be human? That his humanity was only an episode in his existence? The defenders of the kenosis doctrine would answer that it is not a question of his ceasing to be God when he entered human life. The objections pertain to the metaphysical realm and to that area of the relationship between the Father and the Son which are outside the concern of the New Testament. The kenosis doctrine is concerned with the Incarnation. It asserts that God in his great love sent his Son into the world to carry out his eternal purpose of redemption. It maintains that the Son for our sake became poor, that he did not insist

---

[21]Cf. Vincent Taylor, *The Person of Christ in the New Testament Teaching* (New York, 1958), pp. 260 ff.

on retaining his form of God, but emptied himself in taking on the form of man. If this Incarnation was to be real, he had to accept the limitations imposed on human life on earth—physical, mental, and spiritual. He did make this great sacrifice, and the New Testament records the life and ministry of the man in whom men came to perceive God.

The mystery of the person of Christ cannot be explained by our reason or logic. That he was true God and true man is a confession of faith, which is not dependent on any one theory or doctrine attempting to explain it. But since we must think of him in some form, we must try to arrive at a solution which is true both to the biblical witness and to life as we experience it. The New Testament is not concerned to explain the mystery from a metaphysical point of view but only to assert that he was truly man, sharing with us the limitations of human life, and at the same time truly God and therefore able to redeem humanity out of the power of sin, death, and the devil. If it is true that he was really human, that he walked by faith, that he had to find the will of God step by step and day by day, and that as a result he was sometimes perplexed even to the depth of his agony in Gethsemane, he is certainly very close to us and to what we experience as human beings. Then truly we have a High Priest who is "able to sympathize with our weaknesses," for he, too, has walked his way through life in faith and obedience as we must.

# 5.

# Redemption in Christ

## THE DEATH OF CHRIST

The death and resurrection of Jesus is the central theme of the New Testament record. Fully one third of each of the four Gospels is devoted to the story of the Passion and the Resurrection. This is the center of the message in each Gospel to which the rest of the narrative forms an introduction. The Gospels differ considerably in their selection of incidents from the ministry of Jesus, but the Passion story is told in all four in the same order and almost in the same words. This portion of the tradition was evidently the first to receive a fixed form. Recollections of incidents from Jesus' ministry circulated in separate units, but the Passion story was told from the beginning as a connected whole.

The early sermons recorded in Acts bear witness to the same emphasis on the death and Resurrection. The outline of these sermons is always the same: Jesus of Nazareth, whom you crucified, God has raised from the dead. He has made him Christ and Lord; repent, for only in his name is there salvation and forgiveness of sin. (Acts 2:14-36; 3:12-26; 4:8-12; 5:30-32; 10:34-43; 13:16-41). Paul is in complete agreement with this emphasis. In chapter 15 of First Corinthians, he sums up the entire gospel which he preached to his converts, and by which they have been saved, in terms of Jesus' death, burial, and resurrection.

The New Testament is equally emphatic in its assertion that his death was vicarious, that it was "for us." "Christ died for our sins"

(I Cor. 15:3). He is "the Lamb of God, who takes away the sin of the world" (John 1:29). He "gave himself for our sins" (Gal. 1:4). He was "offered once to bear the sins of many" (Heb. 9:28). Since the New Testament declares that he was the sinless Son of God, he should not have been subject to death, but he the "righteous [died] for the unrighteous, that he might bring us to God" (I Pet. 3:18).

It is of course true that the whole life of Christ was vicarious. He came into the world for our sake. His task was "to preach good news to the poor . . . to proclaim release to the captives and recovering of sight to the blind, to set at liberty those who are oppressed, to proclaim the acceptable year of the Lord" (Luke 4:18). His ministry is characterized by the parable of the shepherd who goes out to seek the lost sheep. The vicarious quality of Christ's ministry is most evident, however, in his death. The ancient warning had been: "In the day that you eat of it you shall die" (Gen. 2:17). "The wages of sin is death" (Rom. 6:23). If he were to "bear the sins of many" and "take away sin," it would involve his death. All his life was vicarious, but the church understands that the central element in his work "for us" is his death and Resurrection.

The church was originally faced with the unexpected and baffling fact that although the Messiah had come, he had suffered and died, risen again and returned to heaven. What did this event mean for the relationship between God and man? Here was a new and stupendous act of God, a new event in the history of God's dealings with humanity, and it was necessary both to proclaim and interpret it. The event had happened, but what did it mean? There were no obvious precedents for the church to follow. In its attempts to interpret this new event the church had to draw on the resources of the Old Testament, the teaching of Jesus, and the guidance of the Holy Spirit. In order to make the Christian claim intelligible, the leaders of the church had to use whatever conceptions were at hand in the Old Testament, in the teaching of Jesus, and in the experience of the men they were addressing.

The situation which confronted the church was quite obvious.

Humanity had fallen into sin, but God had a plan for salvation. The hostile power that had come into the world to corrupt God's creation was to be destroyed and eliminated. God was to establish his everlasting kingdom in righteousness and peace. But what would really be necessary in order that sin should be removed and righteousness established? How was the death and resurrection of Christ related to this "taking away of sin"? This was the problem which faced the New Testament church and which had to be interpreted to the world.

The answer provided in the New Testament is not given in one consistent conception or in one stereotyped form. It varies according to the writer and the situation from which he was speaking. Thus in Galatians, Paul declares that Christ has set us free from the law and its observances, that salvation is by grace alone through faith, and that any insistence on circumcision and such observances as a condition of salvation is a denial of the grace of God. Here Paul is writing in answer to the demand of the Judaizers for compliance with the law of Moses. In Colossians, he is thinking in terms of heavenly powers and angelic beings, or "the elemental spirits of the universe," and here he declares that whatever powers there may be in heaven, on earth, or under the earth, Christ is the supreme Lord over them all, and he has set men free from their authority. In Second Corinthians he has vividly in mind the reconciliation that Titus has effected between him and the congregation, and thus he speaks of the work of Christ as a reconciliation between God and man. The local situation determines to a large extent the form of the answer. These answers are not logical explanations but suggestions of how the work of Christ might be apprehended. The mystery of Christ's death had to be interpreted, but it remained a mystery even after an explanation had been provided. The answers take the form of parables and metaphors that permit us to apprehend the mystery, even though we do not fully understand it.

One of the answers given in the New Testament was that the death of Christ was a *sacrifice for sin*. The idea of sacrifice is found among practically all peoples. Among primitive peoples, if a person wants to succeed in an important undertaking, he had better invoke the help and favor of the gods by some offering or sacrifice that will prove acceptable. And if a person has committed an offense, so that the gods are angry, he must propitiate them in some way. If it was a serious offense and possibly involves the whole people, the sacrifice must be something that is especially dear to the person or persons involved—thus a human sacrifice of a son or daughter, even of a king, may be demanded. So deep-seated is this conception that even many Christians attempt to render God favorable by means of self-denial, offerings, prayers, pilgrimages, fastings, and gifts.

The conception of an angry God who must be pacified and rendered favorable by man's efforts is a heathen idea which has no place in the biblical narratives. It is true that the Bible speaks freely of judgment and the wrath of God, but this wrath is the consistent and determined opposition of God to the forces of evil that threaten to destroy his creation. It is neither capricious nor malicious. It is a part of God's purpose to redeem and restore his creation.

Man need not and cannot, therefore, render God favorable to himself by his own efforts. God is favorable to man. In his love he takes the initiative and comes to seek and to save the lost, and to bring man into fellowship with himself.

Nevertheless, man is separated from God, a sinner and a rebel. He is unclean, so that he cannot stand in the presence of a holy God or be used in his service as he now is. His iniquity must be removed and his uncleanness washed away, and only God can provide the means for it. The Old Testament means was sacrifice for sin. In offering this sacrifice the person admitted his guilt, accepted the judgment of God upon himself, and trusted in the means provided by God to bring about an atonement. The sacrifice contained the three elements of judgment, redemption, and promise we saw involved in God's confronting man. The judgment is carried out on the vicarious victim with whom the offerer identifies himself, and the unclean person is cleansed and becomes the object of God's renewed blessing.

The sacrificial character of the death of Christ is conceived of in  this sense in the New Testament. Here God's judgment on sin was carried out. God has "put [him] forward as an expiation by his blood" (Rom. 3:25). Possibly we should translate *hilasterion* here "mercy seat," as in Heb. 9:5, instead of "expiation." The mercy seat was the lid of the Ark of the Covenant, over which God was invisibly enthroned, where he manifested his glory, and on which the blood of the sacrifice of the Atonement Day was sprinkled. All these ideas are present in the passage in Romans. In Christ God has manifested his cleansing and expiating mercy, not in the secret of the Holy of Holies, but publicly on the Cross; not in the dim light of the sanctuary, but on a hillside outside the city; not in the sprinkling of "alien blood," but in the blood of the Only Son. All the ideas of the Old Testament sacrificial system, and all the means provided in the past for cleansing and making men holy, find their fulfillment in this sacrifice that was made once for all on the Cross.

The death of Christ is described as a sacrifice in several passages in the New Testament. There is certainly a suggestion of it in the words of institution of the Lord's Supper: "shed for you for the remission of sins." John's Gospel says that Jesus will give himself for the life of the world. In the Letter to the Hebrews the interpretation of his death as a sacrifice is carried out in great detail. Paul's saying that "Christ, our paschal lamb, has been sacrificed" (I Cor. 5:7) also clearly points in this direction. The beautiful passage in I Pet. 1:18-19 speaks of "the precious blood of Christ, like that of a lamb without blemish or spot." These passages indicate that the early church understood the Cross in terms of a sacrifice for sin through which man was cleansed and prepared to stand in the presence of God. Man is unclean, he is washed "in the blood of the Lamb," and thus becomes holy.

A second interpretation, which is also common in the New Testament, is that in his death Jesus *suffered the penalty for our sin.*

This interpretation, of course, is implicit in the idea of vicarious suffering, which plays a prominent part in the account of the Suffering Servant in chapter 53 of Isaiah. We may well hesitate to say that God inflicted the penalty of sin upon him, for the prophet, too, suggests that those who saw his suffering *mistakenly* assumed that he was "stricken, smitten by God, and afflicted." It was man who crucified him, not God. Yet the Crucifixion was in accordance with the eternal counsel and foreknowledge of God. If suffering and death are "the wages of sin," then somehow he must have suffered the penalty of sin for us. The idea of responsibility for one's action is built into the very structure of man's universe. No one really expects to escape the just punishment of sin. While man's sense of moral order may be hopelessly corrupted and perverted, there remains nevertheless a feeling of responsibility and a sense of justice. If he was "made to be sin for us," then in some sense he also suffered the consequences of sin.

When this conception is perverted to mean that God was angry and demanded that someone must die, or that he would not, or could not, show mercy until the last ounce of punitive suffering had been extracted, it becomes a denial of the whole fundamental message of the Bible. The biblical conception of the penalty does not mean that God had to inflict suffering on an innocent victim before he could show himself merciful, but rather that in his infinite love God himself in Christ takes the penalty upon himself on behalf of man.

 A third, and even more common, interpretation in the New Testament is that Jesus' death was a *ransom*. This metaphor is used especially by Paul. It is taken from the institution of slavery and the practice of manumitting slaves on the payment of a ransom. The figure is therefore simple and effective. Man is a slave under alien powers—sin, death, and the devil—and Christ's death is the ransom for man's freedom. Stated rather crudely it might be said that God's creation was lost, God buys it back (re-deems it) at the price of the blood of Christ, and thus creation is restored. Jesus declares that he has come "to give his life as a ransom for many"

(Mark 10:45). Paul tells the Corinthians, "you were bought with a price" (I Cor. 6:20). Peter says "you were ransomed [bought back] from the futile ways inherited from your fathers, not with perishable things such as silver or gold, but with the precious blood of Christ" (I Pet. 1:18-19). Those who had been slaves under such alien powers as sin, law, and death were now redeemed into "the glorious liberty of the children of God." This is an answer to the question of the meaning of Christ's death which has brought freedom and joy to all generations of Christians. Like all figures, it must not be pressed too far. When questions are asked to whom the ransom was paid, what it was for, and why it was necessary, the whole conception ends in fruitless speculations. His giving himself "a ransom for many" was not a commercial transaction. Although the New Testament is content to use this figure for interpreting the death of Christ, the term ransom remains a metaphor, an analogy, not an exact or literal explanation.

There is a fourth conception of the Passion closely related to the  ransom metaphor, namely, that the Cross represents a conflict and *a victory over the evil powers.* A captive can be released by defeating rather than paying his captor, as Jesus suggests in explaining his exorcisms by the parable of the strong man and him who is stronger (Luke 11:21-22). He was sent "to proclaim release to the captives" (Luke 4:18). Paul expresses the same thought when he says that Christ "disarmed the principalities and powers and made a public example of them, triumphing over them in him" (or, "in the cross") (Col. 2:15). Jesus has come "to destroy the works of the devil" (I John 3:8; cf. Heb. 2:14). The final victory comes when death is abolished and the devil is "thrown into the lake of fire" (Rev. 20:10).

This conception of the redemptive process is in line with the whole biblical perspective. God contends against the same enemy from Genesis to the final consummation. He does not have to buy the souls of men from their foe. This is God's creation, and the devil has no real title to anything. He is a usurper, an interloper, the enemy who has sown weeds among the good grain and cor-

rupted the good work of God. He must be eliminated: deprived of
his power and destroyed by "the stronger" who takes away the
weapons in which he trusted and his goods as well. The disciples
saw in the death and resurrection of Jesus a victory over this alien
power or powers. Since Jesus was now "both Christ and Lord," he
would shortly return and manifest his complete victory.

Finally, a fifth figure sees the work of Christ as *reconciliation* between God and man. Sin has caused a separation between God and
his creatures that has resulted in a state of hostility and enmity. Man
is opposed to God and hostile to his will. The hostility is not only
between God and man, but also between man and man. Christ
has come to remove the hostility, to effect a reconciliation, and to
establish peace. The emphasis here is on the result of his work
rather than on the act itself. The reconciliation may of course be
effected by his sacrifice, by the payment of a ransom, or by suffering
a penalty. The figure does not really say how it was done, but simply that "God was in Christ reconciling the world to himself" (II
Cor. 5:19). He did whatever was necessary to remove "the dividing
wall of hostility" and thus reconciled "us both to God in one body
through the cross" (Eph. 2:14-16). Since separation and hostility
represent a mutual relationship, both God and man were involved.
But it is God who in Christ takes the initiative to effect reconciliation.

We must realize that these answers are in the form of metaphors,
figures of speech, and not exact, logical, and systematic explanations. We say that Christ's death was a sacrifice, and we know what
a sacrifice means. It is an offering presented to a deity. But does
this explain the death of Christ? There is an obvious analogy, but
how does his death affect a person of another generation? The figure of the payment of a ransom becomes crude and misleading as
soon as we ask some pertinent questions. How can one person take
upon himself the guilt of another and suffer the penalty for him?
This is not permissible in the administration of even human justice,
according to everything we have learned about the nature of justice!
"Warfare" without swords, guns, or bombs is a very strange war-

fare, not to mention that one of the contestants is the God who is supposed to hold all power in his hands. No matter how much the Bible emphasizes the reality and seriousness of the struggle, this seems to render it almost a sham battle. The New Testament uses these figures, and they are tremendously suggestive, but they do not solve the problem. The mystery remains. It apparently is not in the theoretical sphere but in the experience of the new life which we find in the Christian community that we know that Jesus "was put to death for our trespasses and raised for our justification," and the various images we use are only feeble attempts to describe that for which there is no exact analogy.

The one common aspect in all these figures is the *cost* of redemption. Whether we think of sacrifice, the payment of a ransom, suffering the penalty, or warfare, the suggestion of all these images is that the cost involved was infinite. "God so loved the world that he gave his only Son." The cost was the life of the Son of God, "who loved me and gave himself for me" (Gal. 2:20). The cost of redemption was not borne by man but by God himself. Judgment strikes the sinner, to be sure, but God is the ultimate sin-bearer and pays the price of redemption. Even the Incarnate Son was appalled and in dread over the cost, and prayed that there might be some other way to achieve the purpose of God. There apparently was no alternative. He had to drink the cup and pay the price for the redemption of man.

Our difficulty in interpreting the death of Christ is increased by the fact that we isolate the event instead of seeing it in the whole context of God's revelation. We take too narrow a view of the Cross. If we look at it only as a point in time, a few hours of struggle under the darkened skies of Golgotha, it becomes an event in the past to which we look back as something already finished. We come to regard God's activity prior to that event as merely preparation and waiting, and his activity afterwards only as the application of this event to subsequent generations. If the Cross is the key to God's redemptive acts in history, we ought rather to let the Cross define God's activity both in the past and in the present. God is the same yesterday, today, and forever.

If our interpretation of the redemptive biblical events is correct, we have to see the Cross as the revelation in time of God's constant, redemptive activity. God did not begin here on the Cross to redeem the world, nor did he finish. He began as soon as sin entered the world, and he will continue until the purpose is fulfilled and the kingdom is established. The people of Israel were really God's people in the Old Testament, and they were so, not by virtue of what was going to happen in the future, but by God's act of redemption, and because he was their God right then. He told them, "I am the Lord your God," and they said, "He is our God, and we are the people of his pasture and the sheep of his hand" (Ps. 95:7). It is true that they were a sinful and rebellious people, but God was at work among them to redeem and give life. Although this redemptive activity was in a different form and not yet fully understood, it was nevertheless of the same nature and significance as the work of Christ. The very fact that the New Testament can use the Old Testament for guidance in its interpretation of the death of Christ indicates that the activity of God is essentially the same in all ages. Even if the people of the Old Testament did not fully understand this, we are to see God's past activity in the light of the Cross. The Cross illumines and interprets the acts of God in the past and reveals his eternal purpose to redeem his creation and destroy the enemies of life. It tells us, not only what God did at one point in history, but what he was also doing before to realize his purpose.

In a similar sense the work of God in the present is a continuation of the work of Christ, under a different form and in a universal sense. God meets us now in the proclamation of the gospel of Christ to redeem, set free, reconcile, and make alive. Paul wrote his converts that "even when we were dead through our trespasses, [God] made us alive together with Christ . . . and raised us up with him" (Eph. 2:4-6). He said that "God was in Christ reconciling the world to himself," but he also added, "We beseech you on be-

half of Christ, be reconciled to God" (II Cor. 5:19-20). This reconciling work is now going on wherever the gospel comes. Just as
Christ triumphed over all the evil powers, so now "in Christ" and
by the operation of the Spirit we are released from bondage to
these powers and set free. Wherever and whenever man is brought
back from the far country to the Father's house, it is by an act of
God in Christ.

It must not be inferred that by placing the death of Christ in the
context of the whole activity of God we thereby minimize the significance of the Cross. All of God's acts are decisive in the context
in which they occur. We are rather trying to see the whole perspective of God's acts in history in terms of his redemptive purpose.
In whatever form we think of the work of Christ, we must realize
that all acts of God can be described in similar terms. If the Cross
was a conflict with evil powers, so also were his actions in the redemption and election of Israel. If we think of it as a sacrifice or
suffering for sin, we must realize that God ultimately suffers for all
sin. If God is love, as the New Testament says, he must suffer
when his creatures turn against him, spurn his love, and rebel
against his good and gracious will. The Cross reveals and defines
the activity of God from beginning to end.

The Cross, however, is more than a revelation in time of God's
continuous activity. It is a part, and a decisive part, of that activity.
The Cross was real suffering, real sin-bearing, and a real conflict.
It was in fact unique, since here the Son of God himself as a man
took upon himself the sinfulness of humanity and suffered its consequences. We need not curtail or discount the New Testament
witness to the centrality and decisiveness of the act of God in
Christ. He is the Savior, Suffering Servant, and Redeemer for all
time. But he did not begin this work at the time of the Incarnation
(or of his baptism), nor did he finish it with the Ascension. Since
he is the same yesterday, today, and forever, he is also today the
One who redeems and gives life. It is not a question of minimizing
his work, but of extending the conception of it to cover not only
the mid-point but all points along the time-line of God's eternal

purpose. He is "the Lamb of God, who takes away [not "took away"] the sin of the world."

The conception of the continuous work of Christ may be seen also in the fact that the sufferings of the saints are closely related to the sufferings of Christ. His suffering does not eliminate the sufferings of those who belong to him. Paul is intensely concerned that he may "share his sufferings, becoming like him in his death, that if possible I may attain the resurrection from the dead" (Phil. 3:10-11). As the Cross defines the activity of God from beginning to end, so the Cross also defines the Christian life. The struggle goes on. There are still Satan, sin, the old man, and death, which have to be overcome daily. We may include here the sufferings of the saints in the Old Testament, for they, too, were conscious of the intense struggle that had to be endured. If in some sense the Suffering Servant stands for the people of God, then their suffering, too, is vicarious. Paul says, "I complete what is lacking in Christ's afflictions for the sake of his body, that is, the church" (Col. 1:24). There is a price to be paid for redemption. God's forgiving grace is free, but it is not cheap. There were no short cuts to the messianic goal for Jesus, and there are no short cuts for us to the promised land. The sign of the Cross does not stand on Golgotha only, it is the sign that stands over the whole of God's dealings with humanity and over the life of every Christian.

## THE RESURRECTION OF CHRIST

### The Problem of the Resurrection

The resurrection of Christ is a difficult problem both for the the theologian and for the preacher. It is proclaimed in the New Testament as the greatest of all events and the most powerful of God's acts. Jesus was "designated Son of God in power according to the Spirit of holiness by his resurrection from the dead" (Rom. 1:4). Paul's summary statement of the kerygma (I Cor. 15:3 ff.) includes only three things: that Jesus died, was buried, and "was raised on the third day in accordance with the scriptures" (italics added). The emphasis on the fact that he lives pervades the whole New Testament.

The preaching of an Easter sermon is in many respects the most difficult task facing the preacher. Since it is really true that a person who was crucified, dead, and buried rose from the dead on the third day and lives forever, the event is unique, and the most remarkable event in all history. Even if it be declared in all the superlatives that language affords, anything that is said falls far short of being adequate and meaningful. After the simple account found in the Gospels has been read, what more can be said? This is the greatest of all victories over man's ancient enemy, death! The hymns of the church are filled with exultant expressions of joy over this event on the third day. Since it is asserted that he rose again and lives forever, the event is of an eschatological nature.

The greatness of the event tempts the preacher to make assertions that are unrealistic and irrelevant. He is apt to maintain that the enemies of man have been defeated and destroyed; that sin, death and the devil have lost their power; that the new day has dawned and the new age has come. The statement that Christ in his death and resurrection has destroyed sin, death, and the devil has found its way into the confessions of faith in some churches, and would naturally therefore be repeated in the Easter message. A realistic appraisal of the conditions in the world belies such a claim. Skeptical spirits in the early church are reported to have asked: "Where is the promise of his coming? For ever since the fathers fell asleep, all things have continued as they were from the beginning of creation" (II Pet. 3:4). It may even be plausibly argued that the Easter victory made no appreciable change in the conditions of human life in this world. Sickness, suffering, cruelty, oppression, toil, trouble, and death have been just as common since that time as before it. We have already pointed out that the New Testament speaks realistically of the power of the devil and of his activity in the world. Man's inhumanity to man has continued in the subsequent centuries. The cruelty of the inquisition in the Middle Ages and the horrors of the gas chambers where thousands of men, women and children were exterminated in our own day are eloquent testimonies to the power of evil that captures and controls mankind. What evil men do to one another can be seen clearly in the ruins of Hiroshima and in the devastation of the cities of Europe. To proclaim in the face of these conditions that sin, death, and the devil have been destroyed, as though they have lost their power and cannot operate any more, is unrealistic and therefore irrelevant. It is not sufficient to say, as Cullmann does, that "the conquered powers still possess a certain strength."[1] The New Testament bears witness to their continued great power, and our common human experience testifies to the same fact. It would be tragic if the Easter message were proclaimed in such a way that actual conditions refuted the claims of the preacher.

The theologian has another problem to face: The message of the resurrection is contrary to all human experience. The answer to the old question, "if a man die, shall he live again?" is, as far as human experience goes, a categorical "No." There is a flippant saying that nothing in this world is sure except death and taxes, a statement of human experience. No matter how strong the will to live may be, or how successfully a living thing may overcome great obstacles for a time, ultimately every living thing dies, and the universal human experience is that once dead, it stays dead. The biography of a man ends at death, and therefore many of the written "lives of Jesus" end with the Crucifixion and the burial. The theologian—and, of course, the preacher is also a theologian, who must interpret the significance of the Resurrection and its relevance to the present day—the theologian must affirm the resurrection of Jesus in opposition to this universal experience of humanity.

The resurrection of Jesus, however, is not proclaimed as merely the resuscitation of a once-dead body, or as simply the return to life of a person once dead, as in the case of Jairus' daughter, the young man in Nain, or Lazarus of Bethany. According to the Gospels, these persons returned to life, yet they were not freed from death;

---

[1] Cullmann, *The Early Church*, p. 156.

they would presumably die again later. The resurrection of Jesus, on the contrary, was an eschatological event. He passed out of the power of death into life: from this life into the life to come. He prayed, "Father, the hour has come; glorify thy Son that the Son may glorify thee . . . Father, glorify thou me . . . with thy glory which I had with thee before the world was made" (John 17:1 ff.). The Resurrection is the preamble, the first fruits, of that final event to which all creation looks forward. He has been "highly exalted," "seated on the right hand of God," and "given a name that is above every name." What has happened with him is a preview of what shall take place in the final restoration of all things. In Cullmann's words: "In Christ, according to the Primitive Christian faith, only his own body had previously risen to become a spiritual body. Other spiritual bodies do not as yet exist."[2] In him the Spirit has already taken full possession of the body and completely penetrated it. This is the first fruits of the new creation that is to come with "new heavens and a new earth" (II Pet. 3:13). Such theories, therefore, as have been advanced to explain the disappearance of the body of Jesus on the basis of analogous experiences have no relevance to his resurrection. The New Testament saw this event as a preview of what is to happen at the end of time. The Resurrection was an act of God, an eschatological event, through which he rose into that life which is the goal of all human existence in the purpose of God.

Since the resurrection of Christ was an eschatological event, the question of the empty tomb is not properly a subject for historical determination. It would be so only if we assumed that the Resurrection was simply a resuscitation of a dead body and marked a return to the previous conditions of life. It is an event that lies, as it were, on the border-line between time and eternity. The New Testament reports the empty tomb and emphasizes the identity between the crucified Jesus and the risen Lord. At the same time, Paul's analogy of the grain of wheat that dies and rises again to a *new*

---

[2]Cullmann, *Christ and Time*, p. 141.

mode of life must be remembered here. The transformation of his body into the new state of glorification was the act of him who "makes all things new."

The eschatological event is at the same time a historical event. We have seen that the Bible presents the acts of God as historical happenings. God's activity is *in* the world although it is not *of* the world. God operates in history to advance his purpose and redeem his creation. The Resurrection occurred in historical time, on the third day after the Friday of the Crucifixion. Sunday became in the early church the day of the Resurrection, as Friday was a day of fasting in commemoration of the Crucifixion. Even though, as we will discuss later, the proclamation of the event of Christ in the church means that we die and rise with him, the Resurrection is not a timeless event. It took place at a certain point in time in accordance with "the determinate counsel and foreknowledge of God."

The faith of the early church, like the faith of Israel, was a recital of God's acts in history, and it included "the third day he rose again from the dead." We cannot surrender faith in this event as an actual, historical act of God. To do so is to surrender also faith in his death as the redemptive act of God. "If Christ has not been raised, then our preaching is in vain and your faith is in vain." "If Christ has not been raised, your faith is futile and you are still in your sins" (I Cor. 15:14, 17). His death and Resurrection belong together as two facets of the one event; one cannot be accepted without the other. "The *kerygma* is a *kerygma* about Christ's death and resurrection, both in one, bound together, indivisible."[3]

There is a tendency to isolate the Resurrection from the other events connected with the life of Jesus. Many accept his ministry as a work of God, possibly even the Incarnation and his death as a saving event in God's dealing with humanity, but reject the idea of the Resurrection as an actual event, or place it in a category analogous to the immortality of the soul. When the latter is done it is

---

[3]Wingren, *op. cit.*, p. 128.

affirmed that Christ lives, but the body is left aside. The New Testament reports the Resurrection to be an actual event. The tomb was empty. "He is not here, for he has risen" (Matt. 28:2 ff.; Mark 16:4 ff.; Luke 24:2 ff.; John 20:1 ff.). It is not sufficient to say that this represents the faith of the early disciples, and then to try to suggest plausible explanations for their arriving at this faith. The historian is satisfied with registering that the early disciples believed that Jesus had risen from the dead, which is as far as he can go in his role as a scientific historian. It is not his task to answer whether this was true or not. The preacher and the theologian, in so far as they are Christians and stand within the presuppositions of the Christian faith, cannot avoid the question of the truth of the disciples' belief. The theologian deals with the problem of the relationship between God and man, and this relationship is profoundly dependent on whether the death of Jesus was merely a human event or belonged to the saving acts of God. Nor can he accept the death and leave aside the resurrection, because the two are integral parts of one event. He cannot affirm that God was in Christ reconciling the world to himself, and then refuse to accept that God also raised Christ from the dead.

The affirmation that Christ died and rose again is a confession of faith. We have emphasized that the claim that these events are acts of God and a part of his eternal purpose cannot be established by either historical or scientific arguments. The people concerned in these events experienced and interpreted them as acts of God, and subsequent generations have lived and experienced the reality of this confession in their own lives. It may be freely admitted that the Resurrection stands in a class by itself, since it partakes directly of the nature of the final, eschatological event. Death is a universal human experience; the Resurrection is unique. The Resurrection is, in fact, contrary to all human experience and to everything we have witnessed in the fields of biology, chemistry, and medicine. The analogy that nature dies in the fall and rises to new life in the spring, which is the basis of the nature myths in pagan religions, is not pertinent here. Nature does not really die in the fall, and the appearance of life in plants and flowers in the spring of the year is simply a reawakening to a new cycle of life. Whatever in nature really dies stays dead. The resurrection of Jesus was a final, eschatological event: Christ does not die again, death has no more dominion over him.

Since the Resurrection is an article of faith, it cannot be adduced to prove either that Jesus was the Son of God or that his death was an atonement for man's sin. We cannot prove one article of faith by citing another article of faith, as Bultmann observes.[4] The New Testament does not attempt to prove that Christ has risen from the dead, but proclaims this message as an event that has taken place in which God has acted in a unique and final way for the salvation of men. This proclamation is the witness of the original disciples to the Resurrection. They affirm that it really did happen, and that they saw the risen Lord after his Crucifixion and death. The one whom they saw after his death was the same one with whom they had walked in Galilee, whom they had seen and heard, and whom they had come to believe was the Messiah of God. This witness of the disciples rests on their own experience of seeing the Lord. Their testimony forms the basis of the preaching of the church, in which Christ confronts men today as the crucified and risen Lord. Our faith is the same as the faith of the original disciples, faith in him through whom God has acted to destroy death and "bring life and immortality to light through the gospel" (II Tim. 1:10).

The New Testament never assumes that the death and Resurrection of Jesus were events *likely* to happen—certainly not the Resurrection. The disciples were astonished at the announcement by Jesus that the Son of man had to die and be raised on the third day, and wondered "what the rising from the dead meant" (Mark 9:10). That the Son of man should suffer and die, even to rise again, was as repugnant to them as to the rest of the Jews. It was the event itself and their own experience of it that con-

---

[4] R. Bultmann, "New Testament and Mythology," in *Kerygma and Myth* (London, 1953), p. 40.

vinced them he was indeed the living Lord. In reality their belief was not very different from the basic belief that God is active in the events of human history. That it was God who called Abraham, redeemed the people out of Egypt, and returned the Exiles was also a matter of faith. The whole biblical perspective is a confession of faith, one which may be rejected as visionary and unreasonable, but one in which men have found the answer to life's deepest problems. For him who stands aside and demands proofs, the Bible remains a curiosity and a possibility, but nothing more. The message is to be proclaimed and accepted in faith.

## The Significance of the Resurrection

As we suggested above, in the Easter proclamation the temptation is strong to assert more than is warranted by the New Testament. The idea of the D Day may overshadow the final V Day. The claim that man's ancient enemies have been destroyed, that their powers are now more limited than before, or that the victory already has been won goes beyond the New Testament proclamation. In the New Testament the final victory and the elimination of all opposition to God is still in the future.

What then was the victory of the death and resurrection of Christ? What is the Easter proclamation? It is the message of the personal victory of Jesus and of his exaltation as the "Lord and Christ." He has passed through death and lives forevermore. "The death he died he died to sin, once for all, but the life he lives he lives to God" (Rom. 6:10). The Letter to the Hebrews insists that Christ made his offering in his death "once for all when he offered up himself" (Heb. 7:27). He did not need "to offer himself repeatedly, as the high priest enters the Holy Place yearly with blood not his own; for then he would have had to suffer repeatedly since the foundation of the world. But as it is, he appeared once for all at the end of the age to put away sin by the sacrifice of himself" (Heb. 9:25-26). He has performed his sacrifice once for all, and it is unrepeatable. "For Christ also died for sins once for all, the righteous for the unrighteous, that he might bring us to God, being put to death in the flesh but made alive in the spirit" (I Pet. 3:18). Both Paul and the author of Hebrews assume that after he has once died, death has no more dominion over him. "He who has died is freed from sin." "For we know that Christ being raised from the dead will never die again; death no longer has dominion over him" (Rom. 6:7,9).

As the vicarious Suffering Servant, Christ took man's sin upon himself and "was made to be sin" in our behalf. He entered voluntarily into man's situation and took up the struggle against the "principalities and powers" that held man captive. This was a part of the struggle that began in Genesis. He, the God-man, met death and lives. He has won the victory. It was *his* personal victory. *He* lives. *He* is not subject to death any more. This is the jubilant confession of the New Testament people, that he died and rose again, that he has been exalted to the right hand of God, and that he has been given a name that is above every name. In this victory he stands alone. It was his personal victory; death no longer has dominion over *him.* This is the victory message of Easter, and *for him* it was final.

His victory over death, therefore, makes him the Lord of life. He is "the stronger" who has entered into the stronghold of "the strong man," has taken away the weapons in which he trusted and his goods as well. Since one man has met death and emerged victorious, death no longer has the last word. In this universe in which all living things must die, one has lived and died, yet lives forever. He is the Lord of life and of death, and in his hands are "the keys of Death and Hades" (Rev. 1:18). He holds this position by virtue of his victory over "the principalities and powers" (Col. 2:15). His exaltation to the right hand of God means that he rules and reigns, and that all things are subject to him. "All authority in heaven and on earth has been given to me" (Matt. 28:18).

His victory was a vicarious victory *for us.* Since he is the victor over death and is the Lord of life, "having received from the Father the promised Holy Spirit" (Acts 2:33), he can give life to those who belong to him and trust in him. "For as the Father raises the dead and gives them life, so also the Son gives life to whom he will" (John 5:21). He was raised "for our justification." His victory is prophetic of the final victory over death. He is the first-fruits, the guarantee that not death but life is victorious. The biblical record had always asserted the ultimate victory of God. That victory has now been demonstrated in God's mighty act of raising Jesus from the dead, He lives and gives life to all who belong to him.

The Resurrection also means that the Christian must enter the struggle in the name of the risen Lord to participate in the victory. The war is not ended, and the evil powers have not been destroyed. The New Testament pictures realistically how precarious is the existence even of those who belong to Christ. Paul's certainty that the Christian is free from sin means, not that he is sinless, but that he is now in a position to fight against sin and overcome it.[5] Even though the Christians have "died to sin" (Rom. 6:2), Paul nevertheless exhorts them to "put off the old nature" (Col. 3:9) and to put away all the vices that characterized the old life. In spite of the power of evil, the victory is possible. He is optimistic that his converts will forsake their evil ways and walk "in newness of life." His optimism is not based on any belief in the impotency of the enemy, nor yet on his assessment of the personal strength of the individual Christian, but solely on the power of the living Lord. They who are "in Christ," can in him do all things. They are to put on "the whole armor of God, that [they] may be able to withstand in the evil day, and having done all, to stand" (Eph. 6:13).

The struggle goes on and the stakes are high—life or death. In the struggle between God and the devil, man is never a mere spectator: he is involved on one side or the other. The victory of Christ has been won, but our victory is still to be achieved, now and on the last day. The closing words in each of the letters

---

[5]Nygren, *Commentary on Romans,* trans. Carl C. Rasmussen (Philadelphia, 1949), pp. 230 ff.

to the seven churches in Revelation are similar to: "He who conquers, I will grant him to sit with me on my throne, as I myself
conquered and sat down with my Father on his throne" (Rev. 3:21.
Cf. 2:7,11,17,26; 3:5,12). The promise in each case is to the
one who conquers. Neither the victory of Christ on the Cross and
Easter, nor the victory of Christians in their new life, is final.
There is something lacking, something yet to be done. Christ reigns,
but he reigns in order to put all his enemies under his feet.

It is difficult to keep a proper balance between now and not
yet: we are saved, we will be saved; the kingdom has come, the
kingdom will come. It is easy to be pessimistic about the present
and to put all the emphasis on the victory on the last day. This
viewpoint has sometimes been emphasized to such an extent that
any attempt to improve present conditions or to work for a
better social order have been regarded as futile and even contrary
to the will of God. On the other hand, the victory of the Resurrection has sometimes been interpreted as the only decisive event
in God's redemptive work so that nothing more need be done.
As is so often the case, the realistic position of the New Testament
takes both the present and the future seriously. The enemies are
strong—the struggle is serious, and the dangers are many—but
there is nothing final about their power. Their finality was lost
when One went through death into life. The Christian looks to the
living Lord and is assured that death itself shall be "swallowed
up in victory." Death does not have the last word. That belongs
to him who says: "I am the Alpha and the Omega, the beginning
and the end" (Rev. 21:6).

When we take this view of the New Testament event of Christ,
we are taking the whole biblical perspective into consideration.
We can then allow the Old Testament its proper place as an
account of the redemptive activity of God. Every act of God is
decisive, and in a sense eschatological and final, for it takes place
in the context of God's whole purpose and design. The event of
Christ Incarnate takes its place within the whole history of salvation, as an event in the developing purpose of God. Yet Christ is

not confined to any one point: he is the Lord over the whole process from beginning to the end. We who live now may regard ourselves as united with all those who have heard the Word of the Lord and experienced his redemptive power. We, too, are called to participate in the conflict and to enlist in the ranks of those who by the Spirit of the living Lord fight the battles against man's ancient foe. We look back in faith to what God has done in the past, and we look forward in hope to the fulfillment of the promise. We walk by faith as Abraham did, as Jesus himself did, confident that "he who began a good work in us will bring it to completion at the day of Jesus Christ."

# 6.

## Living under Law

### GOD'S ACTIVITY IN THE PRESENT

We have now surveyed the story of the great biblical events in which God has revealed himself as the present and active God whose will and purpose is to redeem and restore his fallen creation. These events culminate within the historical record in the incarnation, death and resurrection of Christ, while in addition, the Bible points forward to a new event and a final consummation, which is designated as the return of Christ. This sequence of events reveals God's ultimate purpose for humanity and his creation.

In concentrating our attention on God's activity in these particular events, and in speaking of God's "invading human history" on these occasions, we do not assume that God is active only at certain moments of crisis in history, nor that in the intervening periods the world is less subject to his direct will and rule. When we say that man always stands between the events of the past and the promise, looking back in faith to what God has done and forward in hope to what he will still do in the future, we do not mean to minimize the present nor to claim that man's attention should be directed primarily toward the past or the future.

Such conclusions would be entirely erroneous and contrary to the biblical record. These events are significant precisely because they reveal God's steadfast purpose and declare what God is doing continually for the salvation of man. God is the living God, and the record of his acts in the past is significant for us because it reveals his character, his purpose, and his intention in reference to man's existence now in the present. On the basis of studying and analyzing the record of God's acts in the past, we proclaim that God is the same yesterday, today, and even forever.

At this point, therefore, we shift our attention from the biblical record of the past acts of God to a consideration of what it means that God is continuing the same activity in the present. God comes to man in this modern generation just as he came to the first rebels, Adam and Eve, to Noah, to Abraham, to the slaves in Egypt, and the people of the first century, and he comes for the same purpose. The proclamation of the gospel in all its ramifications is the form in which God's activity appears most clearly in the present.

Just as the coming of God in the biblical events involved the three factors, judgment, redemption, and promise, so his coming today in the preaching of the Word confronts man with the possibilities of death and life. God rules the world in judgment and in grace, in destruction and in giving of life. The struggle in which he is engaged involves the defeat of the enemy and the release of the captives to freedom and blessedness.

We will discuss the present activity of God, therefore, from two points of view, which we may designate as judgment and redemption, or, using the technical terms, law and gospel. Luther speaks of the two "realms": the government by God's left hand, the law, and the government by his right hand, the gospel. This distinction could be misleading if suggested that "the left hand" were less important than "the right hand," or not as directly a work of God. It might be preferable to speak of God's rule as Creator and his rule as Savior and Redeemer. In either realm, it is God who acts, and the whole creation is the object of his concern and is comprised within his purpose and activity.

When, for the purpose of discussion, we divide the activity of God into these two categories, law and gospel, or judgment and redemption, we must remember that both are God's direct activity in the world and both have the same purpose of preserving and redeeming his creation. He does not deal with some men through the law and with others through the gospel. All men are subject to God's law, and all are comprehended within his beneficent concern and redemptive purpose. They live in the world and must participate in all the affairs and activities which belong to mankind in general, and in this context they encounter also the presence of God as the sovereign Lord and the gracious Redeemer. Every man receives his life from God and lives under God's authority whether he recognizes and acknowledges this fact or not. When Paul in Rom. 1:18 ff. describes man's rebellion against God and his failure to "honor [God] as God and give thanks to him," he clearly implies that this rebellious man remains under the power and authority of God. This relationship of every man to God, which no one can sever, may be described from the point of view either of law or of gospel.

In the present chapter we are concerned with "the law" as an expression or vehicle of God's activity in the world. God rules his whole creation in accordance with his will, and he has established the conditions under which life exists. The laws according to which everything comes into being and moves are not simply mechanical, or arbitrary, or autonomous; they are the expression of God's sovereign will and of his design for all that exists. In the next chapter we shall discuss God's redemptive activity in the present, through which he now carries on the work of reconciliation.

## THE LAW IS GOD'S LAW OF CREATION

The universe is created and sustained in accordance with God's will and plan. Everything that exists moves according to laws that he has established. Modern man knows that nothing in this vast expanse is at rest. The great heavenly bodies as well as the constituent parts of the smaller atom are constantly in motion in relation to one another. Just to continue in existence such a universe must include law and order. If only one major part departed from its orbit, there would be destruction and chaos. The universe is in fact so orderly, law-abiding, and dependable that man can observe its movements and predict far in advance when astronomical phenomena will occur. When certain conditions are met, man can confidently predict the outcome.

As man learns to know more and more of the mysteries of the world in which he lives, he finds that everything is made to live and move in accordance with a given pattern. He discovers how the universe works, and he formulates the principles he finds constant and dependable. The principles of order do not originate in man's mind; they are man's tracing out of the laws the Creator himself has established for his work. Law, then, is not primarily a code, or a book, or a collection of statutes but a statement of God's will according to which he has determined that his creation shall exist and move. Law is not something that man imposes on existence, either physical or social; it is the principles and realities man has found inherent in the existence of his universe.

*Physical Law*

The evidence for a law of creation is obvious in physical nature. In the physical realm everything moves in accordance with the law laid down in creation. Man has always been impressed by the spectacle of the starry heavens and the planets which move in orderly procession across the firmament night after night. The ancients spoke of "the music of the spheres" and of the celestial harmony that prevails in the universe. As our knowledge of the universe expands, the total effect of its magnitude and order is overwhelming. If a psalmist with limited knowledge could say: "The heavens are telling the glory of God; and the firmament proclaims his handiwork," how much more should modern man be impressed by the glory and power of him who created all these things! Our knowledge of the universe has become so tremendously detailed and complex that to conceive of a being who is the maker of it all and superior to it all is almost an impossibility. Yet the deity has always been conceived of as greater than man

can ever fathom, as a *deus absconditus,* and Jews and Christians
have long asserted that God is wholly Other, one who dwells in
light unapproachable. The Bible recognizes the vastness of the
universe and still maintains that God is supreme over all, and
that he is concerned with his creation (cf., e.g., Isa. 40:21 ff.;
Ps. 8:3-4).

In the cosmic realm God's will seems to operate without opposition. The stars in their courses follow the orbits set for them.
As far as we know, God's rule is unchallenged in all the vast im-
mensities of this universe. It appears that "It is only a spiritual
being, endowed with the power of choice, who can possibly go
against God's will"[1] and destroy the order in God's creation. Man's
ability to interfere with the physical order is limited, even though
he has now discovered powers in atomic energy which could, if
they were released in one great intercontinental struggle, destroy
all life on his planet.

As a part of the physical universe, man is subject to very strict
laws. He is conceived, is born, and develops in accordance with
predetermined biological laws. If he is to live, he must eat, sleep,
and exercise, for example, and do so in a certain moderation. If
he violates any biological or hygienic laws, he must suffer the
consequences. He has, of course, a certain latitude here, since
he can choose to disregard these laws to some extent, but he is
basically subject to the laws of the physical universe and must
obey them, even when he does not know or understand them.
Far from being impersonal rules or arbitrary commandments, these
laws are the conditions according to which God has determined
life here on earth. Furthermore, these laws are universal and
applicable to all living creatures. Within certain limits these
laws operate inexorably. It is either obey or perish.

## Social Law

God's will and law operates also in human, social life. God has
created men—and even the forms of higher animal life—as

---

[1]Edwyn R. Bevan, in *The Kingdom of God and History,* p. 39.

social beings who must live in communities with one another. A
person is dependent for his very conception and existence on a
social, sexual action involving two persons. When God says, "It
is not good for man to be alone," the reference is not simply to
the companionship of a woman and the propagation of the race;
God has created man to be a social being who must live in fellowship with his neighbors. "No man lives to himself." There is no
self-sufficient human being, for each one depends at least upon
the parents who have given him birth. The higher the biological
order of a creature, the greater his dependence on his fellow
creatures. A young animal becomes independent in a relatively
short time, but a child depends on its parents for many years. On
a primitive level a man might live for a long time independently
by fishing, hunting, and tilling a little plot of ground, but in
any culture more highly developed he is dependent on the social
structure for the everyday necessities of life.

It is in the social realm that opposition to God is most serious.
Since man is a spiritual being endowed with will, he has more
extensive freedom here than in the physical realm. Instead of
living in peace with his neighbor he can become antisocial,
determined to destroy God's creation and his neighbor. Although
man is created by God, he is also a sinner and a rebel against
God's will. In spite of his rebellion he remains subject to the
laws, both for the physical and for the social life, that God has
established for man's existence in the world. Physically he must
conform to the normal development of a human being, and socially
he must take into account the neighbor and the community in
which he dwells, its customs, mores and ordinances. Man has
a free will, but he can exercise this free will only under very
strict limitations.

## THE LAW OF LOVE

The law which God has established for man's spiritual and
social life is summed up in the Bible in two great commandments
as love to God and love to neighbor. "You shall love the Lord

your God with all your heart, and with all your soul, and with all
your mind. This is the great and first commandment. And a
second is like it, You shall love your neighbor as yourself. On
these two commandments depend all the law and the prophets"
(Matt. 22:37-40; cf. Deut. 6:5, Lev. 19:18). This, says Jesus, is
the sum and substance of the law and the prophets, i.e., of the whole
Scripture. Paul expresses the same idea when he says that man's
fundamental duty is to "honor [God] as God and give thanks to
him" (Rom. 1:21), and again, "For he who loves his neighbor has
fulfilled the law. The commandments, 'You shall not commit adultery, You shall not kill, You shall not steal, You shall not covet,'
and any other commandment, are summed up in this sentence, 'You
shall love your neighbor as yourself' " (Rom. 13:8-9). Again
Paul says, "The whole law is fulfilled in one word, 'You shall love
your neighbor as yourself' " (Gal. 5:14; cf. Jas. 2:8).

The first, fundamental law of human existence is that man shall
recognize and "honor God as God and give thanks to him." Man
owes his existence to God and is utterly and completely dependent
on his will. The life that man enjoys is a gift of God. Man is a
dependent creature; he does not have "life in himself" as God has.
The primary duty of man is to recognize this state of dependence
and give thanks to God for his gift. If we think of the biblical perspective and the purpose of God revealed in it, we may say that
man is to find his place within this perspective and purpose, and
come to an understanding of himself *(Selbsverständnis)* within this
context of the will and purpose of God.

Man's fundamental sin is to deny his dependence on God and to
seek to establish himself in the world as an independent being. He
wants to be "like God" instead of recognizing God as God and as
the ultimate ground of his being. Man cannot be independent.
When he attempts to be independent, the result is disaster. Instead
of becoming independent of God he becomes dependent on powers
that are not God, and he makes for himself idols to which he pays
homage (Rom. 1:22-23). The moral degradation of which Paul
speaks in the first chapter of Romans is the result of man's refusal

to recognize the revelation which God has given to him through "the things that have been made." Through his refusal to recognize God as God, man becomes a slave under alien powers: sin, death, and the devil. If he is to be saved, he must be brought back to an acknowledgment of his actual state of being as dependent on God.

Sinful man must give up his rebellion and recognize God as God. The commandments are prefaced by the words, "I am the Lord your God," and again, "Hear, O Israel: The Lord our God is one Lord" (Deut. 5:6, 6:4). This is a statement of a fact of man's existence, the fundamental truth of life. There is no possibility of escape from this fact. God is God whether man recognizes it or not. Nor is this in any sense a partial relationship which applies only in certain areas of man's life. It involves man's whole being— heart, soul, and mind. Man's dependence on God is total and involves all of life.

Man's duty to God is then simply to recognize God as God and himself as a being created by God. Man cannot give anything to God or be profitable to his maker. "Truly no man can ransom himself, or give to God the price of his life" (Ps. 49:7). The relationship between God and man is really a one-way relationship; God is the giver and man is the recipient of his gifts. All man can do is recognize this fact of his existence and "honor God as God and give thanks to him." The acknowledgment may, of course, be expressed in those forms of worship through which man in his long history has tried to express his sense of dependence on God. Very often even worship becomes corrupt, degenerating into an attempt to coerce God into granting his favor and blessing. Both the prophets and Jesus denounced corrupt worship as an abomination in the sight of God. Nevertheless, we may surely see in these ceremonies, even when corrupt, a sense of acknowledgment of man's consciousness that he owes his life and existence to a higher power, though his conception of this power be woefully inadequate. Paul implies that all men have this knowledge of God as Creator, but it is in the biblical tradition that God has truly revealed himself as "the Lord your God."

"You shall love the Lord your God." The word love, however, has become so freighted with sentimental and erotic connotations that it now fails to express the true relationship involved. It becomes necessary to define the content of this term in the light of the relationship between God the Creator and man the creature. What does love to God imply? Some claim that "love" is not generally used to express the relationship of an inferior to a superior. In the past, while a man "loved" his wife, her relationship to him was expressed by such words as obey, reverence, serve. In the Bible there are relatively few passages where man is the subject of the verb "love" and God is the object. The prominence of this summary of the commandment creates the impression that the usage is more common than it really is. The commandment, however, must mean primarily that man recognizes God as Creator and Lord and acknowledges his utter dependence on his Maker. The terms, therefore, that are generally used to describe man's relationship to God are to obey and to trust, or to be faithful. God is the Creator who is infinitely concerned for his creatures, and man is therefore to "fear, love and trust God above all things else." This is the meaning of the first great commandment.

The second commandment is the fundamental law of man's *social life* in the world. "You shall love your neighbor as yourself." This commandment expresses a relationship between fellow-creatures. Love in this connection primarily means that man as a social being must be concerned for the temporal and eternal welfare of his neighbor and that he identifies himself with him. There is certainly a measure of sentiment involved here, but it is not the primary element. In the popular sense of the word "love," it is impossible to love some people. They irritate us, they are arrogant, they may even be enemies looking for an opportunity to hurt and destroy us. There is no pleasure in associating on intimate terms with a bore. Nonetheless, it is possible to be vitally concerned for the temporal and eternal welfare of all men, even of enemies. "Love your enemies." God has created us as social beings, to live together in mutual dependence and helpfulness, in harmony and peace. The

fundamental law of man's social existence is that he shall live together with his fellows and be concerned for his neighbor: "Love
your neighbor as yourself."

There has been a great deal of discussion about the meaning of
the addition to the commandment, "as yourself." It has been argued, for instance by Anders Nygren, that "self-love" is incompatible with the doctrine of man's total dependence on God and the
concern for the neighbor. If self-love means to have one's center in
self and to place self first at all times, it is certainly the very oppo-
site of the spirit of the commandment. Jesus' words in the Sermon
on the Mount about turning the other cheek, going the second
mile, and giving to him who asks imply a disregard for one's own
interests in favor of service to the neighbor. Obviously, if the neighbor is to be the center of concern, the self cannot be the center at
the same time. Nygren writes:

> Agape spells judgment on the life that centers around the
> ego and its interests. . . . As Christ "pleased not himself," we
> also as Christians "ought . . . not to please ourselves," but "let
> each of us please his neighbor for that which is good" (Rom.
> 15:1-3; cf. Phil. 2:4). When in passages like these Paul sets
> self-love and neighborly love in opposition to one another, he
> is not condemning merely a lower self-love, or the natural ten-
> dency to self-assertion, but all self-love whatsoever, even in its
> most highly spiritual forms.[2]

True concern for the neighbor ends with the neighbor; this, according to Nygren, is the *agape* of which the New Testament speaks.

It is, of course, true that even service to the neighbor may be
done in the interest of self. Jesus mentions those who sound the
trumpet before them in the street when they give alms (Matt. 6:2).
The gift may be for the neighbor, but it is given to reflect favorably
on the giver. If we approach the problem from the point of view
that God has created man as a social being, the sharp antithesis between neighbor and self may be resolved. Each man is part of a
society within which every individual acts and reacts upon the

---

[2]Nygren, *Agape and Eros*, trans. Philip S. Watson (Philadelphia, 1953), pp.
130-131.

others. The common goal is the welfare of all, including every in-dividual. No one stands apart from this social order, and each one has his place, his prerogatives and his obligations. That the help given to the neighbor may return some advantage to the one who gives help is almost inevitable within this social structure. Right social conduct benefits the whole community, including the one who performs any specific act of service to the neighbor. When we see both neighbor and self as a part of this social structure in which each is dependent on the other, the apportionment of benefits to the neighbor and to self becomes less important. It remains true that the motive for action should not be concern for self, but concern for the welfare of the neighbor and society as a whole. Parents, for instance, may urge their children to study so as to receive good grades; if the children do so, it brings a cherished reward to the parents. Yet the parental love cannot be dependent on their mak-ing good grades nor do true parents urge the children to study in order that they themselves may receive the obvious or more subtle benefits. They are concerned about them just because they are their children. In the same way each one in the social structure has to consider the welfare of the neighbor just because he is a neighbor, not because this active concern may bring a reward, which it some-times does and sometimes does not. If a merchant or an industrial concern wants to be successful in business, for example, the firm will have to be interested in the service it can render to its customer and the well-being and morale of its its employees. The very struc-ture of social life determines that no one can be concerned for self alone; it implies that each one has a place in the social structure and finds the fulfillment of his life only in a vital relationship of concern for his fellow men.

Jesus and Paul say that the commandment of love to the neigh-bor expresses the whole will of God for man's social life. From this fundamental statement are derived every legitimate commandment and law to be found among men, whether in the biblical tradition or in the tradition of other cultures and peoples. Since God has created man as a social being, man is obliged to live in a community with his fellows, and his life must be regulated by various laws and ordinances. From the point of view of Jesus and Paul, and in accordance with God's intention, all laws, ordinances and regulations have only one purpose, to establish and safeguard a social order in which each man must be concerned for the welfare and well-being of the neighbor and of society in general. This is the fundamental law or principle which God has incorporated into the very structure of his creation of man as a social being. The law applies to all men, and it operates in community life whether man recognizes it as a commandment of God or not. God has made man in such a way that he cannot exist except in a society, and that he must be concerned to maintain order and harmony in all his relationships with his neighbor.

Not all human laws and regulations are in agreement with this intention of God. Since man is a sinner, he has distorted the social life. Man's laws, institutions, and governments sometimes become so corrupt that they no longer serve God's purposes. Man has made laws to protect the powerful, oppress the poor, or give privileges to a few and discriminate against others. Laws have been applied to minority groups in order to keep them in subjection. In these areas, too, man's rebellion is in evidence. Just as man wants to be independent of God, so he tries to make himself independent of his fellow men and, if he is powerful enough, exploit them for his own interests. The law of concern for the neighbor remains the fundamental law of man's existence as a social being, and the disregard of it ultimately breeds discontent, revolution, and chaos.

This law of concern for neighbor is so fundamental that it takes precedence even over observances intended to honor God. The commandment about love to neighbor is not in any sense inferior to the first commandment or of less importance. In his teaching about the Sabbath, Jesus declared that the Sabbath was made for man, not man for the Sabbath, and he defended his disciples when they were accused of breaking the commandment in order to satisfy their hunger (Mark 2:23-28). A vow like Corban must not be allowed to hinder a man from helping his parents in need (Mark

7:9-13). If a man who is on the point of performing his worship or sacrifice remembers that he has a disagreement with his brother, he must first go and be reconciled to him before he offers his gift (Matt. 5:23-24). To respond to human need and to come to the assistance of the neighbor constitute man's fundamental responsibility.

Since God has created man a social being, all vices and all virtues are social. Sin is sin *against* someone, either God or the neighbor. A person destined to live forever alone on a desert island would be free to act as he pleased. The only sin he could really commit would be to curse God and kill himself; even so, it would be a sin in relation to God. It is impossible to kill or steal—certainly to commit adultery—except in relation to someone else. All sin is social, and it always involves defiance of God's fundamental law of concern for neighbor. Thus the Psalmist must say: "Against thee, thee only, have I sinned," even though his sin was against his neighbor.

Sin, then, is ultimately selfishness. Man sins when he becomes antisocial, i.e., when he sees the presence of the neighbor as a limitation on his desire to realize his own selfish ends. In Sartre's play *No Exit,* one line is "Hell is other people." From man's selfish point of view this is true, because the presence of the neighbor imposes a limitation as well as an obligation on man. If a man were the only one using a highway, he could drive as he pleased, but since there are other people using it also, he must stay in his own lane. Men can drive along the highway at great speed only because they are confident that all others will observe the law. There is, of course, an element of self-preservation in observing regulations, which is intimated in the addition "as yourself." If concern for the neighbor cannot be entirely purged of concern for self, it is also true that concern for self always leads to some concern for the neighbor. Since man is a part of the social community, he is included in the general concern for all the members.

This law of concern for neighbor is universal and imposed on all men in whatever society they may live. All men must live in a social structure where the neighbor must be served. The law operates

negatively to restrain men from doing evil to their neighbor. This
is Paul's conception of government in Romans 13. Society has to
protect itself against the forces that destroy life. The government
is thus an institution ordained by God to ensure that this law of
concern for neighbor shall be properly observed. The government
does this by punishing the evil and rewarding the good. If a man
insists on dumping garbage in the alley, the sanitation department
steps in and he may be fined for his action. When the government
embarks on a welfare program, it is carrying out on a large scale
the injunction of concern for neighbor. Whether it is in a primitive
tribal society, or in the complex order of a modern city, the same
law of concern for neighbor applies.

These laws, customs, mores, governments, and social agencies,
therefore, in so far as they promote the general welfare, are an expression of God's will for his creation. God is the God of all peoples, whether they know it or not, and he is concerned for all. There
is no profane world, no profane law; it is God's world and God's
law in so far as it is designed to protect life and make men serve
one another. Men may do this voluntarily, recognizing that God
is God and acknowledging his will, or they may be compelled to do
so by the pressure of human society, but no man can be a member
of any community without taking into account its customs and
mores and being concerned for others. God has laid down this law
in the very structure of his creation and in the nature of man, and
he has made this so plain that no normal human being can ignore
it. Most men seem to know and recognize that violating the life of
another or refusing to help a neighbor is wrong. When Jesus in the
Sermon on the Mount included not only the overt acts of murder
and adultery as contrary to the commandment but also the inward
desire, he expressed the fundamental law of concern for the welfare of the neighbor. When this concern is the guiding principle
of life, man cannot even desire to violate his neighbor's rights and
life.

This interpretation of the commandment may seem to demand
a complete suppression of the individual in favor of society. At the

present time a great many protests are raised against conformity and "the organization man." Here as elsewhere it is difficult to keep a proper balance. What this law of love to neighbor means, however, is not the suppression of the individual, but the *fulfillment* of himself and the realization of all his powers in service to God and the neighbor. The individual has to be himself, but he can be a self only within the social structure, which is inherent in God's creation of man as a social being. Only in obedience to these fundamental commandments can he realize the full meaning of his life and attain to his true stature as a man created by God. The individual has a right and a duty to assert himself and insist that society itself recognize and obey the law of concern for all men. In a sinful society, where laws and institutions may be made to serve vested interest and power groups, the individual must raise his voice in protest. Injustice and unrighteousness can become accepted customs and laws. The prophets of the Old Testament are splendid examples of men who denounced the wicked kings, judges, and priests because they oppressed the poor and rendered unrighteous judgments. How far the individual may go in his protest must be determined by each one for himself. In any case he must be guided by his own conscience and be "fully convinced in his own mind" (Rom. 14:5). He must also be willing to accept the consequences of his actions and his failure to conform.

It is clear, therefore, that what this commandment of concern for neighbor demands in any given situation must be determined in the light of all the attendant circumstances. The Bible sets down the principle or law that man must be concerned for the temporal and eternal welfare of the neighbor. But what does the welfare of this particular neighbor involve, and what should be done? The Good Samaritan found a man lying half dead along the road and he did what at that time and in those circumstances had to be done. In these days if a man is found lying in the road, hit by a car, the police must be notified and an ambulance secured. A man crazed by drink may have to be restrained, overpowered and put in jail. The will of God is clearly expressed in the law of concern for neighbor, but the answer to what should be done in every given case cannot be provided in a code. The Old Testament represents the customs and mores of the early Israelites, most of whose rules and regulations have become obsolete. What should be done in any given case cannot be decided before the case arises. The Good Samaritan came "by chance" this way. When "by chance" the needs of the neighbor are presented to us, the commandment indicates, our desire to meet them must precede the means, for the measure of our response is determined by the degree of our absorption in self, which can prevent the need of the neighbor from being registered in our consciousness or assessed with sensitivity. The more complex society becomes, the more difficult it is to know the needs of the neighbor and to take adequate measures to meet them. When merely individual response becomes inadequate, society as a whole, even the government, has to enter the welfare field. The church, voluntary associations, and the government are all concerned in this work. Whatever our attitude toward the modern welfare state, we must recognize it as the modern response to the ancient law of concern for the welfare of the neighbor. It, too, can become corrupt, but the pressure on the government to care for the welfare of all its citizens must be recognized as the operation of God's fundamental law for social life. The church has a place in this work, for it is concerned for the welfare of the whole man: body, soul and spirit.

## THE CHRISTIAN AND THE LAW

God's fundamental law of creation is one for all men, believers and unbelievers, Christians and pagans. Since all men are created by God, they should all recognize and honor God as God. Because man is created a social being who must live together with his fellow men, everyone must be concerned for his neighbor. The implications of these two commandments may not be very clearly apprehended among men in general, but even in the most primitive societies there is some recognition of man's dependence on God or the gods and some acknowledgment of responsibility for the welfare of other men. The clearest and most consistent revelation of the spirit and content of these two commandments has been given in the Bible and especially in the New Testament. The Bible gives only an amplification and elaboration of these laws which are inherent in God's creation. "On these two commandments depend all the law and the prophets" (Matt. 22:40).

Since man rebels against both God and his neighbor, he distorts and corrupts these fundamental laws of his existence. He defends his selfishness by insisting that everyone must look out for himself first—who else is going to do it? He enacts bad laws, and then maintains that he is acting lawfully. If he is able to take care of himself, he insists that everyone else should do the same. Even while doing these things, however, he knows in himself that he is in the wrong. Paul declares that all men show "that what the law requires is written on their hearts, while their conscience also bears witness and their conflicting thoughts accuse or perhaps excuse them" (Rom. 2:15). The consciousness of sin, which Paul attributes to all men, bears witness to the fact that God is the Creator and that he has made man a social being who feels the requirement to live with his fellow men and be concerned for their welfare. Such a knowledge of the will of God is universal, and the feeling of guilt, therefore, is also universal.

Paul has also declared that man has been freed from the law, as the woman whose husband is dead is freed from the law concerning the husband (Rom. 7:1 ff.). The freedom from the law was Paul's special concern. Jesus taught that man must disregard man-made laws when they came into conflict with the concern for human welfare, or when ceremonies and the performance of ritual acts became ends in themselves, but he did not say that man is free from the law.

Paul's difficulty about the law was due to a large extent to his own experience. Paul had made one great discovery and insight: man is saved by grace alone through faith and not by works of law. "For by grace you have been saved through faith; and this is not your own doing, it is the gift of God" (Eph. 2:8). This was also the teaching of the Old Testament: when Paul wanted an example of a man justified by faith, he went back to Abraham (Rom. 4:3 ff.). God had called, redeemed and chosen his people Israel without any merit or worthiness on their part. If a man is a slave, he cannot set himself free. If he is dead in trespasses and sins, he cannot make himself alive. Only God can redeem and give life.

Before Paul made this great discovery, however, he had been intensely loyal to the way of the law. Again and again he declares that in his zeal for the law he had excelled most of his contemporaries. He believed firmly that the way to God was by obedience to the law. He understood the law in all its details to be an expression of God's will, and he wanted above all things to do God's will. But it was under these circumstances while he was most zealous for the law that he committed his greatest sin, the persecution of the Messiah in the person of his community, the church. The way of the law had led him, not to do God's will, but in the persecution of Christians to oppose his purpose! Now, instead of just saying that he had been mistaken in believing that the law was a way of salvation, he concluded that the law itself was in some sense at fault. The law, as far as he could see, stands in the service of sin, it multiplies transgression and incites to sin. This led him, especially in Galatians, to incorporate the law among the destructive powers that hold man captive, along with sin and death. Sin, law, wrath, and death belong together in the old aeon, just as grace, promise, faith and life belong in the new age. The law is a power from which man must be set free, but at the same time "the law is holy, and the commandment is holy and just and good" (Rom. 7:12). We can appreciate Paul's problem when he encountered the Judaizers who insisted that man must be circumcised and observe the law in order to be saved. This was a denial of Paul's fundamental insight that man is saved by grace, and it foreboded that his converts might return to the bondage from which they had been delivered through faith in Christ. The law seemed to be in the service of sin.

*Man free of the law*

There is indeed a sense in which the Christian is free from the law. In the first place, the Christian's relationship to God is based on grace, not on obedience to the law. Man is a sinner and a rebel who has broken the law. Even if he should reform and try to do better, he would still be a sinner. No law can transform man into something else, it can only show him what he really is. "If a law had been given which could make alive, then righteousness would indeed be by the law" (Gal. 3:21). Even if a man kept the law perfectly, it would show that he already *had* life, not that he *gained* life by keeping the law. On the contrary, the message of the Bible is that God comes to man in grace and mercy, and that he establishes fellowship with man, not on the basis of holiness or obedience, but on the basis of grace. God's gift of salvation is not conditioned on man's efforts at amendment and betterment: it is a free and gracious gift. Man has only to believe in God, i.e., to recognize God as his God and Creator. As soon as man gives up the ancient lie that he can be independent of God, acknowledges his sinfulness, and throws himself unreservedly on the grace of God in Christ, he becomes acceptable to God. Of course, this is not man's own doing, for God takes the initiative in seeking man, and by the power of the Spirit evokes this response in him. Man's relationship to God continues forever on the basis of grace. Man remains a sinner, continually dependent on God for forgiveness and life. In this sense he is free from the law.

In the second place, the Christian is a new creature in Christ and is filled with the Spirit. He has a new nature. The will of the new man is to do God's will. The law now appears in a new light, and the Christian has a new attitude to the law. It is no longer a power outside of himself which demands his allegiance and coerces him to obedience; it is the will of the heavenly Father who is deeply concerned for the true welfare of his children. The Christian is no longer under an outward compulsion, but is guided by his own new nature to do God's will. He has been restored to that state in which God intended him to live; he has found his true being as a child of God, and in that state he is free. We may refer here to an illustration that has frequently been used. A great modern train moves at high speed across the continent, singing as it moves over the familiar course. The great locomotive can develop all its potential power as it pulls the long line of cars behind it. It is free, and it is a glorious sight to behold as it streaks across the land, but if the engineer should suddenly say to himself, "I am tired of seeing the same side of these hills all the time—I wonder what there is on the other side," the train would be in trouble. At a convenient curve, the engineer decides to leave the track and start out on an investigation: can he proceed? The train is free only as long as it runs where it was made to run and is doing what its designer intended it to do. Man can be free only when he is what God intended him to be, and when he achieves the destiny God intended for him.

 In a third sense, the Christian is free because he now has the resources available for doing God's will. The risen Lord and the Spirit dwell in him. He no longer needs to seek a false independence, because he knows that he is a free child of God and entirely dependent on God. Now he can recognize and "honor God as God and give thanks to him." Since he is now under the care and protection of God, and is not preoccupied with self, he can devote his time to the service of the neighbor. He can serve his neighbor in whatever way the Spirit guides him and the need of the neighbor dictates. This is the true freedom: freedom to be and to do what God intended him to be and do. In this state of freedom it is no longer true that "Hell is other people," for in this concern for neighbor man experiences the blessedness of true fellowship and attains to his real self. In losing his life (self), he gains it.

This is the idealized picture of the freedom of the Christian man. Actually the Christian continues to live in this sinful world, shares in the iniquity of society, and himself remains a sinner. As a member of this human society he remains subject to all the laws, ordinances and governments which operate to create and maintain order in society. He must show respect for authority, for the laws that are in force, and for the customs and mores that are acceptable in society in general. It is only when these customs and laws violate the fundamental commandments of love to God and love to neighbor that the Christian must follow his conscience and the guidance of the Spirit in disobedience to "the commandments of men." Although Paul recognizes that man must live under law and be "subject to the governing authorities," he does not invoke the commandments to secure this obedience. He is so certain of the transformation the Christian experiences by the grace of God and by the power of the Spirit that he believes the Christian will do this, not because the law says so, nor because of the pressures of society, but because he lives now "in newness of life."

# 7.

# The Christian Life in the Spirit

## REDEMPTION IN THE PRESENT

God's relationship to his created beings is ultimately characterized by sovereign love. All that he does, including his exercise of law and judgment, stands in the service of his redemptive purpose and is intended to bring man into fellowship with God. Even his government by law and his execution of judgment are ultimately in the interest of the temporal and eternal well-being of his creatures. When Paul declared in Acts 14:17 that God "did not leave himself without witness" among the Gentiles, he based this statement on the fact that God "did good and gave you from heaven rains and fruitful seasons, satisfying your hearts with food and gladness." The revelation of God's goodness and grace is to be found everywhere.

The Bible sees God's redemptive activity pre-eminently in the great biblical events and supremely in the death and resurrection of Jesus. We have, however, rejected an interpretation of the New Testament that would make the event of Christ the only redemptive event, or would insist that all of God's redemptive work was concentrated in the victory of Christ. We have suggested, rather, that God's activity from Genesis to the final consummation is to be understood in the light of this event, and that the nature and purpose of God's redemptive activity in the present is to be defined by the Cross and the Resurrection. There is a tinge of modalism in the view that God has worked according to one pattern in the Old Testament, another in the New Testament, and a third since the days

161

of the first century. God is the same yesterday, today, and forever.

It is true, nevertheless, that in the biblical account the death and resurrection of Jesus together constitute the fundamental act of redemption, the greatest of all the biblical events. The Son of God came into the world to seek and to save the lost. In the realistic view of the New Testament he came to engage man's ancient enemy in mortal combat, to test death's ancient power, and to "bring life and immortality to light through the gospel" (II Tim. 1:10). Through his victory he has demonstrated that he is the Lord of Life, who is able to redeem all who belong to him from death and to give them life. God's struggle against the ancient enemy had gone on from the beginning, whenever and however that beginning took place, and it continues now in the present. Besides the relatively unanimous agreement that God was active in the Old Testament and that he really redeemed his people, we must see this activity also in the life of the church in the present. The story of Acts is not merely, and certainly not mainly, the acts of the apostles, but rather the acts of the living Christ, the acts of the Holy Spirit, and the redemptive acts of God. And the ongoing story of the church, with all its vicissitudes and aberrations, is still the story of the redemptive power of God in the proclamation of the gospel.

As Jesus came in the flesh to redeem man, so he comes to men today in the proclamation of the gospel which has its center in his death and the Resurrection. He meets us as the crucified and risen Lord who invites us to die with him and to rise to a new life. This meeting, this encounter, is the decisive hour for everyone who hears the message. The decisive moment is not in the past, except insofar as it is through his own concluded victory over death that he has been "declared the Son of God in power," who is able to rescue us from death and gain the victory for us. The decisive moment is *now,* today. The crucified and risen Lord meets us today in the preaching of the gospel for the same purpose as he came into the world: "to preach good news to the poor . . . to proclaim release to the captives and recovering of sight to the blind, to set at liberty those

who are oppressed, to proclaim the acceptable year of the Lord"
(Luke 4:18-19).

The terms and figures that are used to interpret the death and
resurrection of Jesus can also be used to describe what happens now
through the preaching of the gospel. We can speak of sacrifice, vicarious suffering of the penalty, redemption and reconciliation not
only in reference to what Jesus experienced in his personal encounter with death, but also in the present, with the difference that it is
a question of our death and resurrection. Man must die, because
the ancient judgment on sin was death, but he may now die with
Christ and rise to a new life.

### THE ORIGIN OF THE NEW LIFE

In the great conflict between God and the powers opposed to
God's will, man is not only a spectator but an active participant.
The conflict must not be understood as if two cosmic forces are
battling for the possession of man's soul, and man stands passively
by waiting to see what the outcome will be. Man himself is the
sinner who is hostile to God and opposed to his will. After the
Fall, God found that "every imagination of the thoughts of [man's]
heart was only evil continually" (Gen. 6:5). Jesus refers almost
casually and as a matter of course to the fact that man is a sinner:
"If you, who are evil, know how to give good gifts to your children . . ." (Matt. 7:11). In any concordance of the Bible entries
under "evil" occupy several columns. In the first section of the
Letter to the Romans, Paul's argument is that all men, Gentiles
and Jews alike, are guilty before God, and he brings in the verdict
from the Old Testament: "None is righteous, no, not one" (Rom.
3:10).

Man, then, is not a being who occasionally does something evil;
he *is* evil. It is not man's occasional acts of sin that make him a
sinner; man sins because he *is* a sinner. Without in any way trying
to explain how this sinfulness is transmitted from generation to
generation, the Bible clearly holds that all men are sinners. This
is a total state. There are no exceptions, and there is no possibility

for man to escape. The church has developed a doctrine of "total depravity," which has sometimes been understood and interpreted in an impossible sense. Although man has fallen into sin, he has not lost his humanity and he remains under the law of God. He must live, as we have indicated in the previous chapter, in fellowship with his neighbors, and he must be concerned with others, if only for the sake of self-preservation. He can never be concerned for himself alone because God has created him a social being. He can rebel against this fact, but only within certain limits. Total depravity, therefore, cannot mean that man is incapable of doing good or treating his neighbor with kindness and respect, nor that all his deeds are evil. As long as man lives in a human society, he is involved in the customs and mores of his society. In this situation some men are better than others, perhaps only better adjusted, or truly more concerned for their neighbor and ready to help. It is in relation to God that all men stand on the same level. They are separated from God, sinners and rebels. This separation is absolute, total, in the sense that man cannot help himself or by his own efforts return to a right relationship with God. There is no "redemption of self by self" in the Bible. The fundamental doctrine is that man is a sinner and that God alone saves and gives life. It is true that man is exhorted to repent and turn to God for forgiveness and life. Repentance is possible only because God takes the initiative in his search for man's true self. Man cannot help being a sinner because he is involved in the corporate sinfulness of the race. In a sense therefore he is not individually responsible for his situation, which is, nevertheless, a situation of lostness. Yet, if he refuses when God comes to him with his offer of grace and salvation, he becomes responsible for remaining in this lost state.

How can the sinful man escape from his state as a sinner and become an obedient child of God? This is the great mystery of the redemptive work of God, which cannot be explained in logical and propositional statements but must be proclaimed in figures of speech that suggest rather than explain the action of God. Just as the interpretation of the work of Christ in his death and the Resurrection had to be made in such figures as a victory over evil powers, reconciliation of enemies, payment of a ransom, and vicarious suffering of the penalty for sin, so the redemptive work of God in the present must be set forth in similar terms. There are a number of such figures of speech in the New Testament describing the old state of sin, God's act of redemption, and the new state of life.[1]

### FIGURES OF SPEECH FOR SALVATION

| The Old State | The Act of God | The New State |
|---|---|---|
| Slavery | Redemption | Freedom |
| Enmity | Reconciliation | Peace |
| Being an alien | Adoption | Being a son |
| Standing accused | Justification | Acquittal |
| Death | Making alive | New life |
| Debt | Forgiveness | Freedom |
| Being cut off | Engrafting | Union |
| Uncleanness | Cleansing | Holiness |
| Being lost | Finding | Homecoming |
| In the flesh | Making to die | In Christ |

It is clear that each of these figures forms a sequence which involves the experience of salvation, the passing from the old state of death into the new state of life. The figure used to describe the old state determines the rest of the sequence. If man is a slave, he must be ransomed or redeemed, and then he becomes free. If there is enmity, there must be a reconciliation, and the result is peace. If man is an "alien," or "afar off," he must be adopted or "brought near," and thus become a member of the family of God. Jesus thought of men "as sheep having no shepherd," and he himself is the shepherd who goes out to seek the lost lamb until he finds it and brings it home to the fold.

By these metaphors the New Testament proclaims and describes the act of God. They do not refer to separate acts of God, as if he were doing a multitude of different acts in carrying out his redemptive work. These figures cannot be arranged in the logical sequence

---

[1] The author has discussed these figures more extensively in *The New Life in Christ* (Philadelphia, 1950), now out of print.

of an *ordo salutis,* as though God first redeems, then reconciles, justifies, adopts, sanctifies, and engrafts. Such a psychological analysis
of the Christian experience of salvation can be a legitimate study
in the field of psychology of religion, but it is not the purpose of
these figures as they appear in the New Testament. They describe
a single act of God in a simple order of salvation involving the old
state, the act of deliverance, and the new state. They are used to
describe what God does for the salvation of man. They are keryg-
matic rather than theological or psychological.

The terms used to describe the old state indicate man's helpless-
ness and his separation from God. A slave cannot set himself free,
a dead man cannot make himself alive, an alien cannot by himself
change his status. The radical nature of man's predicament is indicated by such terms as enmity, dead in trespasses and sins, unclean and lost.

The transition from the old state to the new is, therefore, by an
act of God. God is always the acting subject. God redeems, reconciles, justifies, makes alive, etc. As God was the one who acted in
the great biblical events—in rescuing Noah, in calling Abraham, in
bringing Israel out of Egypt and in returning the Exiles—so it is
God alone who in every generation saves and redeems man. All
the figures emphasize that man is helpless, and that God alone
brings him out of the state of bondage into "the glorious liberty of
the children of God" (Rom. 8:21).

It is important to recognize that this activity of God is constant
and continuous. The redemptive act of God cannot be located at
some point in the past, or the future, either at the mid-point or at
the end-point: it is his constant work. Most of the figures that we
have listed are taken from the New Testament, to be sure, but the
Old Testament describes God's activity in much the same terms.
The people were "in the house of bondage" in Egypt, and God
brought them out by his strong arm. Their bondage was indeed
physical, for they were literally slaves, and the redemptive act made
them God's chosen people. In the vision of the prophet the returning exiles were to be a new people and a fit instrument for

God's purpose. It is true that redemption in the Old Testament remained inseparably connected with the hope of Israel for the possession of the land, but this hope had its center in God, who would redeem and recreate Israel as a people for his own possession.

The past, the historical, is therefore important to us not for itself, but because it portrays the activity of God, which was the same then as now. Bultmann is quite right in his emphasis on the existential moment. "Christ meets us in the preaching as One crucified and risen. He meets us in the preaching and nowhere else. The Easter faith is just this—faith in the word of preaching."[2] But Bultmann's historical skepticism would seem to prevent him from seeing that the record of what God has done in the past is a witness to historical acts which enables us to comprehend what God does in the preaching of the gospel now. If this were not so, there would be no justification for proclaiming the biblical message. The experience of the people of the Old and the New Testament was the same as ours, although they lived under different circumstances and expressed their experience of God's redemptive acts in different forms according to their understanding of the world in which they lived.

The situation of man today is in a way the same as it has been in every preceding generation. Man is still a slave under alien powers, hostile to God and his will, an alien, a rebel, and dead in trespasses and sins. If he is ever to escape this situation, it must be by a redemptive act of God through the preaching of the gospel and the work of the Spirit. That some of the same metaphors apply to the work of Christ in his death and the Resurrection as to the present experience of the Christian indicates that we are dealing with the same activity of God in the past and in the present. When the Christian tries to say what has happened to him now in the present, he naturally likens his experience to the New Testament experiences and expresses himself in the terms of the New Testament. He says that he was a slave under sin, but he is now

---

[2]Bultmann, *op. cit.*, p. 70.

free; that he was lost and is found; or, like the blind man, "I was blind, but now I see." He does not ascribe his transformation to something that has happened in the past, nor to his own efforts, but to the grace of God operating in the present. Wherever and whenever man is brought out of the old state into the new, he testifies that it has happened by a redemptive act of God.

Yet man is vitally engaged in this transition, which is not only by grace but also through faith. When God comes to man, he comes with an offer of life and salvation, which man either accepts or rejects. The prophets demanded that the people of Israel repent and believe in God. Jesus came with the same message: "The kingdom of God is at hand. Repent and believe the gospel." Paul describes the apostolic ministers as ambassadors whose plea is: "Be reconciled to God." When the gospel is preached, man is to believe and obey. The invitation is, "Come to me, all who labor and are heavy-laden" (Matt. 11:28). Man's response is to come, believe, obey, and accept the good news of the gospel.

This action of man is a response to God's activity. God takes the initiative. He goes out to seek and to save the lost. God came to Adam and Eve, to Noah, to Abraham, to the Israelites in Egypt, and to the exiles in Babylon. Jesus came to a lame man at the pool of Bethesda who did not even have the strength to get down in the water at the right time. It is futile to command a lame man to get up and walk without giving him with the command the power to do it. The man heard, believed, obeyed, and got up. The power to rise was given in the word addressed to him. Just so the word of the gospel gives "the power of God for salvation to every one who has faith" (Rom. 1:16), and man is thus enabled to hear and obey. The act of faith means that man is overwhelmed and compelled by the redemptive word of God addressed to him in the gospel, but it means also that man says a timid and yet courageous "Yes" to God.[3] Faith means that man gives up the ancient lie that he can save himself and live independently "as

<hr/>

[3] Aulén, *The Faith of the Christian Church*. trans. Eric H. Wahlstrom and G. Everett Arden (Philadelphia, 1948), pp. 29-30.

God," and that instead he trusts solely in the grace of God in Christ for life and salvation. The redemptive act is an act of God, but man's response is also active and expresses itself in repentance, faith, and obedience.

The origin of the new man or the new life is to be found in the creative and redemptive act of God. God has not abandoned man to his fate as a sinner. Throughout humanity's long history he has been at work to call man back from his rebellion and to bring him into fellowship with God. This is the great mystery of the Christian experience, that man knows himself to be a lost creature, but that he finds in the message of the gospel a way of understanding his own existence and a promise of life.

The abundance of figures of speech to describe the mystery of redemption should make us wary of insisting that the redemptive act must be described in only a certain stereotyped set of terms. The analogy of Jesus as the shepherd who goes out to seek the lost sheep certainly expresses God's great concern for man, but it is not a complete presentation of the act of redemption; although it states part of the truth clearly, that man is lost and that God seeks him, it omits the doctrine of justification by faith proclaimed by Paul not only in Romans and Galatians but elsewhere in his letters. The figure taken from slavery is tremendously impressive and suggestive: man is a slave under alien powers, sin, death, and the devil, but the ransom is paid, or these powers are overcome by "the Stronger," and man is set free. The new state may certainly be described as freedom, but it must also be seen as service to man's rightful Master. The idea of dying and rising with Christ is a partial insight that has been given great prominence in Bultmann's existential interpretation of the New Testament. Christ meets us in the gospel as the crucified and risen Lord in order that we may die with him and rise to a new and authentic life.[4] This figure, like all the others, stands for a reality that is beyond our complete comprehension. The figures are only devices—some

---

[4]Bultmann, *op. cit.*, p. 41.

have mythological connotations from the ancient myths in the religious language of the Near East—but they express, now as then, the reality of God's redemptive act by which he takes a man dead in trespasses and sins and gives him new life.

## THE NATURE OF THE NEW LIFE

The new life of the Christian is a new creation of God. When God calls and encounters men, he creates a new situation and new possibilities for man's existence. The redemption out of Egypt was the creation of a new people who were to have a special history and mission. The Christian is a new creature in Christ. All the figures of speech we have noted indicate that a radical change has taken place through the redemptive act of God. Man was a slave, but he is now free; he was dead, but he now has new life; he was unclean and separated from God, but he is now holy.

There is a decisiveness and finality in this act of God. When the prodigal son returns, he is not put on probation nor told that his status is dependent on his future good behavior; amid great rejoicing he is reinstated fully and completely as a son with robe, ring, and shoes. God's redemptive act translates man out of the old state into the new. When God justifies, man becomes just; when he redeems, man is free; when he sanctifies, man becomes holy. The Christian does not become more free, more just, or more holy later. Once he has been translated into "the glorious liberty of the children of God," he does not become more of a child of God tomorrow than today. The decisiveness of this experience cannot be stated more radically than it is when Paul declares that those who were dead in trespasses and sin have been made alive, and again that he himself has been crucified with Christ and now lives a new life in Christ. God's redemptive act is not gradual, it is decisive and complete.

Still, this act of God includes a promise for the future. The factors in all the biblical events—judgment, redemption and promise—are present also in the individual Christian's experience.

The judgment has been carried out on the old man who had to die. "We know that our old self was crucified with him" (Rom. 6:6). In the redemptive act the sinner dies and a new man in Christ is created. The new creation is not only for the present but for all time: in a sense the redemptive act of God is continuous and eternal. Man has new life, but he has it only as a gift of God. Man is free, but only because God has set him free and keeps him free from the powers that would enslave him. Man is holy, but his holiness is a gift renewed forever. When God forgives, he does so fully and completely, but if he forgives today, he will have to do so tomorrow also. God continues his redemptive work to the final consummation. Salvation is both present and future. It is present, because man knows that he is a new creature in Christ; it is future because God has a purpose and a goal toward which he is working, and his goal involves the destiny of the new man in Christ. The Christian is not only dependent on God for the initial creation of the new life, but dependent also on God's redemptive activity for time and eternity.

The new life created by God is a new, holy, righteous, and godly life. When God redeemed the Israelites out of the bondage in Egypt, their life was to be new and different. They were to be his obedient children, who were to walk in his ways and listen to his voice. At Sinai, and again in the days of Joshua, the people declared that they would serve the Lord and be faithful to his covenant. When the people returned from the Exile, the prophets expected a new age and a new people. The new covenant was not to be like the old broken one, for the law was to be written within their hearts. The people would be "a light to the nations" so that God's "salvation may reach to the end of the earth" (Isa. 49:6).

This conception of the decisiveness and reality of the redemptive act of God and the creation of a new life receives an even greater emphasis in the New Testament. The pattern for the new life is laid down by Jesus in the Sermon on the Mount. The Beatitudes and the principles enunciated here are not a means whereby men are to attain to the new life, but rather the expression of the character and nature of the new life in the kingdom which Jesus has come to bring and establish. The emphasis on the new state is evident in such words as "You have heard that it was said to the men of old . . . but I say to you" (Matt. 5:21 ff.). "For I tell you, unless your righteousness exceeds that of the scribes and Pharisees, you will never enter the kingdom of heaven" (5:20). "You, therefore, must be perfect, as your heavenly Father is perfect" (5:48). The radical character of these words ought not to be blunted by referring them to a state of perfection in heaven. In heaven, presumably no one will need to turn the other cheek, or stand in danger of being sued, or be compelled to carry a soldier's gear a mile or two. The Sermon on the Mount applies to life in the world. But it is a description of a new life, not the old. "The ethic of Jesus, of which the sermon is a summary, is essentially a disciples' ethic. It was given as a way of life for the men in the Kingdom, not for mankind at large."[5] We find the same emphasis on righteousness and holiness in the prophets who believed that Israel was really a new, redeemed people of God, and that they ought therefore to walk in the ways of Yahweh.

Since the Christian has died with Christ and risen to a new life, he must also "walk in newness of life." It was unthinkable to Paul that the new life should manifest any of "the works of the flesh." We can sense from the tone of his Letters to the Corinthians how surprised and horrified he was at the reports that had been brought to him by the members of the Corinthian congregation who visited him in Ephesus. He has heard, he writes, that they quarrel, they go to law against one another, they tolerate and even boast of a person among them who is living in the flagrant sin of incest, and they deny the unity of the body of Christ by their selfish and riotous behavior at the Lord's Supper. All of this denies the reality of the new life. He does not read the

---

[5]Hunter, *op. cit.*, pp. 108-109.

law to them, nor does he quote the ten commandments, but he reminds them that they have been redeemed by the grace of God in Christ, and that the Holy Spirit dwells in them. He addresses them as "those sanctified in Christ Jesus, called to be saints together with all those who in every place call on the name of our Lord Jesus Christ" (I Cor. 1:2), even though their conduct seems to refute this description of them. What they are doing is a part of what Paul elsewhere includes under "the works of the flesh." The Galatians, too, are in danger of going back into bondage to "the weak and beggarly elemental spirits." Their problem is not simply the observance of the law and the practice of circumcision, but their denying the redemptive act of God in Christ and the all-sufficiency of grace by their making the law necessary for salvation and by their "biting and devouring one another."

Paul fully expects that they will change their ways. He cannot imagine that the Christian life could ever be that kind of life. "Those who belong to Christ Jesus have crucified the flesh with its passions and desires" (Gal. 5:24). Sin in the Christian life is abnormal. Sin is one of the evil powers from which man has been set free by the redemptive act of God. The Christian has died to sin and cannot any longer live in it. Sin has lost its authority over the Christian. "Let not sin reign in your mortal bodies, to make you obey their passions" (Rom. 6:12). "For sin will have no dominion over you, since you are not under law but under grace" (Rom. 6:14). When he tells the Colossians "Put to death therefore what is earthly in you" (Col. 3:5), he really expects them to do so. They "have put off the old nature with its practices and have put on the new nature" (3:9-10). These statements of Paul's are just as emphatic and radical as those of Jesus in the Sermon on the Mount. Both Jesus and Paul speak quite concretely and specifically of the vices that are to be put aside and the virtues that are to be practiced. The atmosphere of the New Testament is one of tremendous optimism with regard to the possibilities of the Christian life. It is a new life in the Lord and in the power of the Spirit.

This emphasis on the victory over sin does not imply, either in the Gospels or in the writings of Paul, that the Christian ever becomes sinless. The Chrstian life is still in "becoming," not in perfection. Paul himself makes no claim to perfection, and his letters do not indicate that he had found any of his converts in this state. He was conscious of a struggle in his own life. "Not that I have already obtained this or am already perfect; but I press on to make it my own, because Christ Jesus has made me his own" (Phil. 3:12). He expected his converts to strive against and overcome sin. *Freedom from sin does not mean sinlessness, but the opportunity and ability to strive against and overcome sin.*[6] As long as they were slaves of sin, they were helpless and had to obey its dictates. Now they are no longer slaves, but free in Christ Jesus. The Christian *need not sin,* because sin has lost its authority over him. Just as he previously said "No" to God and to righteousness, he now can say "No" to sin. "Thanks be to God, that you who were once slaves of sin have become obedient from the heart to the standard of teaching to which you were committed, and, having been set free from sin, have become slaves of righteousness" (Rom. 6:17-18). It is true, therefore, that there remains a tension between the flesh and the Spirit even in the Christian life, as Paul indicates in Rom. 7:14-25 and Gal. 5:16 ff. "For the desires of the flesh are against the Spirit, and the desires of the Spirit are against the flesh; for these are opposed to each other, to prevent you from doing what you would" [or "will"] (5:17). Paul assumes that the Christian *wills* to do God's will. The will of the new man is in conformity to God's will, but sin and the flesh are also trying to recapture their mastery over him, and thus the actual performance is not always commensurate with the intention.[7] The Christian is freed to fight against sin, and his struggle is no longer the hopeless struggle of a slave, but the victorious struggle of the free man in Christ. The struggle is serious, but through the grace of the living Lord and by the power of the Holy Spirit

[6]Nygren, *Commentary on Romans,* pp. 241 ff.
[7]*Ibid.,* pp. 292 ff.

there is hope for victory. The description of this struggle in Romans 7 is followed by an emphasis on the Spirit and by the doxology of victory in chapter 8.

This optimistic sense of victory, shared also by the church of the first three centuries, stands in sharp contrast to the pessimism that has characterized the later teaching of the church, beginning perhaps with Augustine. Thus the Reformers developed the doctrine of *simul iustus et peccator:* the Christian is at the same time just and a sinner. In popular understanding and sometimes even in preaching this doctrine has become an excuse for the Christian's failure to live up to the promises and possibilities of the new life. Even if we do not go as far as some opponents of Paul and say that, since we are saved by grace, let us sin in order that grace may abound (Rom. 6:1), the idea lies close at hand. Paul's question "Are we to sin because we are not under law but under grace?" (6:15) is certainly in line with the popular conception that sin is not important because grace covers all. Since the Christian remains a sinner, it is taken for granted that he may sin. Any claim to the contrary, or any suggestion that he can overcome and put away sin, is regarded as an expression of hypocrisy and self-righteousness. Sin in the Christian life thus becomes normal rather than abnormal as Paul regarded it—for Paul answered his own question with "By no means!" When the Christian sins, according to the pessimist, he need only confess: he will thus be assured of forgiveness, for he lives under a blanket pardon, and the grace of God is abundant to cover all his sin. Little more is expected of him than that he should maintain an outward respectability; it is not strange at all that he falls, since he remains a sinner. This defeatist attitude is far removed from Paul's conception of the Christian life.

The doctrine of *simul iustus et peccator,* on the contrary, was not intended to be an excuse for sin or for the failure to carry on a successful struggle against sin. The true meaning of the doctrine is that man is and remains always dependent on the grace of God for salvation and life. The Christian is not partly righteous and

partly a sinner; he is at the same time wholly a sinner and wholly
righteous: he is *totus iustus* and *totus peccator.* The Christian's
righteousness does not depend on his own work or on his own
qualities. He is dependent on grace, not only for his past sins
but for the whole of his life. And even his best efforts and his
most devoted service to God and the neighbor are not works he
can present to God, saying: "At least for these I do not need to
ask for forgiveness." All his life stands under grace and forgiveness.
Luther even dares to say that in this world God's own work is
not perfect.[8] The Christian never comes to a point where grace
and forgiveness lie behind him, where he would have life on the
basis of something other than grace. The righteousness of the
Christian is not his own, it is Someone else's righteousness: it is a
*iustitia aliena.* Even if he hopes to stand someday "faultless before
the throne," he knows that even the hope is a gift of grace alone.
It is only when man acknowledges himself as a sinner who has
no claim whatsoever on God that he can receive the righteousness of Christ. God justifies him "who has faith in Jesus" (Rom.
3:26). This righteousness, too, is complete and total. The Christian
is also *totus iustus,* for God's redemptive act is not partial. "In
Christ" he is fully and completely a child of God, holy and righteous,
but he remains for time and eternity a sinner saved by grace alone.

The doctrine *simul iustus et peccator,* therefore, does not imply
that the Christian can settle back into a state of comfortable secur-
ity. It is, rather, a challenge to realize the potentialities of the new
life. While it is true that the Christian remains a sinner, he is also
"in Christ" and "in the Spirit." Although Paul is the only one in
the New Testament who uses this formula "in Christ," the conception is found in such expressions as "the vine and the branches" or
the shepherd and the flock. There is an intimate union between the
risen Lord and his people. "Where two or three are gathered in my
name, there am I in the midst of them" (Matt. 18:20). It may be
that Paul's formula has a more mystical connotation, but whatever

---

[8]Nygren, *"Simul Iustus et Peccator hos Augustinus och Luther,"* in *Till
Gustaf Aulén* (Lund, 1939), pp. 245 ff.

else it means, it means surely that the Christian life is dependent on the risen Lord. "Apart from me you can do nothing" (John 15:5). The Christian owes not only the beginning of his life, but also the whole of life, to the saving power of Christ. Paul can boast of his work, but he knows that such boasting is foolishness, for whatever he does is done by the grace of God (I Cor. 15:10; II Cor. 11:16 ff.). His confidence of victory rests on the power of the living Lord.

What Paul says about his dependence on Christ is said also of his dependence on the power of the Spirit. The phrase "by or through the Spirit" almost always modifies a verb of action.[9] The Christian lives by the Spirit and walks by the Spirit. "If by the Spirit you put to death the deeds of the body you will live" (Rom. 8:13). "For those who live according to the flesh set their minds on the things of the flesh, but those who live according to the Spirit set their mind on the things of the Spirit" (Rom. 8:5). The clearest passage is Gal. 5:16-18, 22, 25, where Paul contrasts "the works of the flesh" and "the fruit of the Spirit." The works of the flesh are the vices that characterized the old life, and anyone who practices such things "shall not inherit the kingdom of God." But the fruits of the Spirit are love, joy, peace, patience, kindness, goodness, faithfulness, gentleness, self-control. The whole passage implies that the Christians are to put away the vices and exhibit in their lives the quality which is inherent in the new life given to them. That this will involve a struggle is clearly implied, but it is also obvious that Paul expects them to be able to follow his instruction, because the Christian lives by the Spirit and should therefore also "walk by the Spirit." All the resources of the risen Lord and his Spirit are available to the Christian. In Acts 1:8, Jesus promised that his disciples would receive power "when the Holy Spirit has come upon you," and in Acts and in Paul's letters we see how real this power was both in the evangelistic work of preaching the gospel and in the moral life of the believer.

---

[9]Cf. Eric H. Wahlstrom, *op. cit.,* pp. 111 ff.

Since Paul assumes that the Christian life involves a warfare against the power of the flesh, obviously the Christian himself must engage in this struggle. The Spirit does not work automatically, so that all the Christian has to do is to wait for his action. It is the Corinthians themselves who must reform. *You* are to put to death what is fleshly in you, *you* are to walk by the Spirit. The Christian himself is the acting subject. *We* carry on the warfare against "the principalities and powers" (Eph. 6:12). All of the Christian's activities involve this struggle. There is no division of labor between the Christian and the Spirit, so that in some areas the Christian acts by himself and in others the Spirit does his work. Whatever the Christian does in his fight against sin and in his expression of the new life in action is the work of the Spirit, and what the Spirit does is at the same time the work of the Christian. The union is intimate and abiding. The Christian is "in Christ" and "in the Spirit," and the living Lord and the Spirit dwell in him. Something of the same experience is recorded in the Psalms, although not generally in the Old Testament. The gift of the Spirit upon God's people as a whole, not confined to a few chosen leaders, is described in the New Testament as characterizing the period opened up by Jesus' resurrection and exaltation (John 7:39, 16:7; Acts 2:32-33).

Since man is created as a social being, the new life must be lived within the community and under the ordinary circumstances of life. There is no need for a Christian to withdraw from the secular world in order to live in a purely Christian environment, under what might seem ideal conditions. Jesus told his disciples that they were not to be "taken out of the world." They would encounter the hostility of the world, which presupposes that they would remain in the social environment and participate in the various activities of the larger community. The New Testament nowhere expects the Christians to isolate themselves from the world, in which they have a special calling to carry out. The Christian as a new man is now in position to be and to do what God intended man to be and do: to "honor God as God" and to be concerned for the temporal and eternal welfare of his neighbor. He need no longer be anxious about himself, for he is a child of God, under God's constant protection and care. In freedom and joy he can do whatever God gives him an opportunity to do, and do it all "in the name of the Lord Jesus," or in dependence on Christ and the Spirit.

As the Christian lives in the world, he can share also in all that God has created. The idea that the Christian life is circumscribed or fenced in by prohibitions has no support in either the Old or the New Testament. The Bible has a healthy and realistic conception of life in the world. The earth is God's creation, and it is good. It has been created for man to subdue and to use for his sustenance and enjoyment. Man has the privilege of using everything to satisfy his needs, to sustain life, and to further the purposes of God. Work, play, food, drink, sex, laughter, song, and dance are part of the Christian life, as well as thanksgiving and praise. Jesus was always ready to accept an invitation to dinner, even from those who were critical of his activity. He was even accused of being "a glutton and a drunkard" (Matt. 11:19), and he not only attended a wedding but provided wine for the delight of the guests. It is only when the things of the world become perverted from their right use that they become evil and must be classified with "the works of the flesh" which the Christian must "put away." The Bible recognizes man's needs and the conditions of his physical and social life, and it subsumes all of life under the purpose of God and the obedience to Christ. "Whatever you do, in word or deed, do everything in the name of the Lord Jesus, giving thanks to God the Father through him" (Col. 3:19).

## THE REDEEMED COMMUNITY

The Bible proclaims a God who has entered into the world and gathered to himself a people who have heard his voice, experienced his grace, and been elected to serve his redemptive and beneficent purpose. Only a small segment of people is involved in the Judeo-Christian tradition, indeed, but we are to understand this tradition as the revelation of God's universal and constant concern. God is actively engaged in the restoration of his whole creation, and we need not assume that his redemptive activity is limited to what has been revealed to us in the biblical tradition. The Bible itself suggests that "God shows no partiality, but in every nation any one who fears him and does what is right is acceptable to him" (Acts 10:34, 35).

Since man was created as a social being, his redemption involves the restoration of his true life in a fellowship of redeemed men. The enmity which has entered the world through sin and set men against men in ceaseless struggle and conflict has to be removed, and a new order must be established. The laws and regulations of the Old Testament were designed to safeguard the community and to ensure protection and freedom for each individual, the weak as well as the strong. The redemptive act of God creates a community of those who belong to him and live in fellowship with one another. The ideal conception of the Old Testament was that the Israelites were God's people, redeemed by his mighty act and his presence among them, and united into a fellowship of faith and obedience. The New Testament presents the same emphasis on the *koinonia*, a people united with the Lord and held together by a common allegiance to him and to one another.

The church is, therefore, in the broadest outline, the realization of the purpose of God in creation—the society and community which God envisaged for the world. We have already seen that God has established the law of concern for neighbor in the very structure of creation itself. But the goal of community cannot be attained by compulsion and legislation. Man's selfish nature must be changed, and a new man must be created in the image of Christ. Man's rebellion against God and his fellow men must be removed if a new order is to be established. Redemption, reconciliation, regeneration, or whatever term is used to describe God's saving act, has as the result and the goal the establishment of a new social order and a new age. The church is the Body of Christ of which he is the Head, and in which every different part grows together into a unity of mind and spirit.

In a sense at least the church is the new creation, the restoration of humanity, the healing of the fatal flaw introduced by sin. In the fellowship envisaged by Jesus in the Gospels, the selfish striving for honor, prominence, status, and recognition has no place. "It shall not be so among you; but whoever would be great among you . . . must be slave of all" (Mark 10:43-44). The intention of God, expressed in the two great commandments, was to be realized in the new fellowship—love to God and love to neighbor. The social structure established in creation, in which each one is concerned for the temporal and eternal welfare of the other, was to be the hallmark of the new age. "Let each of you look not only to his own interests, but also to the interests of others" (Phil. 2:4).

It may be freely recognized that this new structure has never been fully realized, not even in the small fellowship of the disciples of Jesus. The occasion for the words of Jesus just quoted from Mark's Gospel was the disciples' quarrel about greatness. The history of the church, even in the apostolic age, presents sufficient evidence of selfish ambition and a contentious spirit. The one problem which is raised in every letter of Paul is that of strife, envy, jealousy, and quarreling among his converts. In every letter he has occasion to warn against sins of pride, selfishness, and conceit. Just as the individual Christian remains a sinner and lives by God's forgiving grace, *simul iustus et peccator,* so the church is both holy and sinful, the people of God who live by grace alone. There is no "pure" church.

But when we have granted all this, we must ask: Where in all the world has there been found more selfless devotion to the welfare of others, more earnest concern for the helpless and the destitute, more willingness to redress wrongs and protect the weak, than in the church of Jesus Christ? The church has strayed from the spirit of Jesus even as the disciples did, but it has always retained the power to call its members back to the way of the Master. If the church of today has all the weaknesses of the first disciples and the early church, and even some new flaws of its own, it nevertheless remains the fellowship of the crucified and risen Lord, in which his power to redeem the world still resides.

Since the church is the people of God, it has its ultimate beginning and foundation in the redemptive activity of God. The church is co-extensive in time and space with the redemptive activity of God. It did not begin at Pentecost, nor in the ministry of Jesus, but in the approach of God to fallen man as he called him to repentance and faith. The New Testament was not a new beginning but a continuation of God's redemptive activity which, according to the Scriptures, began at the gate of Eden. While it is true that Easter and Pentecost mark a new development and a new era in the relationship of God with men, they fulfill the Old Testament in the new act of God. It may be said that Jesus founded the church in the sense that God's making him the Messiah created a new situation and made possible a new, universal form for the community, when the Spirit now outpoured could replace the Mosaic law, which had kept the Jews separate from the rest of men; still, his work was founded on the Old Testament and on the work of God already begun. It is always God who founds the church. Wherever it is established and appears, it is the result of his approach to man in grace and redemption.

The church is, therefore, *one* in all ages and in all places. There is only one church, one people of God: those who live by his grace. Social, geographical, or national boundaries need not nullify this unity. The early church had an advantage over subsequent generations in this respect, in that the Roman Empire provided a worldwide unity in which the Greek language was a bond of union, enabling the apostle Paul, for instance, to travel in various parts and proclaim the gospel in a language universally understood. Even in Acts, however, we see the beginning of a division between the Aramaic-speaking East and the Greek-speaking West. When the church spread into other areas, divisions became inevitable. There were Coptic, Persian, Syrian, Greek, Roman, and later Gothic churches. Historical accidents, geographical divisions, the later rise of nationalism, and also the lack of understanding and love, separated the churches from one another. Yet there seems to be no reason a church in a certain country—such as Finland, Germany, or India—should not be administratively independent and manage its own affairs. There is no real reason for denying a group of Christians the right and privilege to form their own organization on the basis of their own traditions and heritage, as long as it does not cut them off from other Christians.

If the church is created and maintained by the redemptive acts of God, then the church comes into being in its entirety wherever the gospel is preached in its purity and the sacraments are rightly administered. A local congregation does not become more truly the church by being organizationally united with other congregations, however natural and necessary such a union might be. Paul addressed his converts as "the church of God in Corinth," or "the churches of Galatia," but there is no indication that they were organized into any kind of synod or federation. The Jerusalem Church, which tried at first to exercise some supervision in Samaria and Antioch, did not succeed (Acts 8:14 ff., 11:22). Although Paul felt free to give advice and counsel, he did not exercise any authority except over those whom he regarded as his own converts. The pattern that emerges in the New Testament is one where the local congregation, although often supervised by the Apostle or his co-workers, conducts its own affairs under its own leadership and regards itself as the true church in any one place. Thus there was from the very beginning a possibility for the development of different traditions and practices in various centers.

The oneness of the church does not necessarily depend either on organization or similarity of rites and customs. The Augsburg Confession declares: "It is sufficient for the true unity of the Christian church that the Gospel be preached in conformity with a pure understanding of it and that the sacraments be administered in accordance with the divine Word. It is not necessary . . . that ceremonies, instituted by men, should be observed uniformly in all places."[10] In

---

[10]*Book of Concord*, ed. Tappert, p. 32.

the nature of the case it would be an impossibility for the church to develop in the same form and pattern everywhere in the world. There are differences in temperament, for instance, between the East and the West—Constantinople and Rome—as there are differences in traditions and history. The development of the modern world has not been the same in every country. The political and industrial revolutions in modern times have not affected the various parts of the world in the same way or to the same degree. The highly hierarchical, authoritarian system that was, perhaps, a necessity in the Middle Ages is an anachronism in a modern, democratic society. Attempts to enforce uniformity have been disastrous both for autocratic leaders, who developed a hard and arrogant spirit, and for the common people subjected to bondage. The unity of the church cannot be established by force, nor even by majority vote.

The unity of the church is to be found essentially in the common allegiance to Jesus Christ as Lord and to the gospel of salvation by grace. Every one of the various branches of the church acknowledges freely that man cannot redeem himself, but must depend on the gracious activity of God in Christ. This basic agreement was emphatically demonstrated at the Conference of Faith and Order in Edinburgh in 1937, when the statement on "The Grace of our Lord Jesus Christ" was accepted without a dissenting vote. Aulén has argued quite convincingly that this central confession of all the churches of the Reformation, justification by grace through faith, is on the way to acceptance as a common confession of the church.[11] No matter how different the churches may be with respect to worship, polity, and emphases on the various aspects of the faith, they would all agree to the basic statement that man is saved by grace through faith in Jesus Christ.

The principal cause of division has been, not the doctrine of grace, but the question how grace is mediated to and received by man. Albeit man is saved by grace, how does it become available? How does God impart his grace and love to man? This question

---

[11]Aulén, *Reformation and Catholicity,* trans. Eric H. Wahlstrom (Philadelphia, 1961), p. 121.

has been answered in various ways. We may distinguish broadly three common emphases: sacramental, evangelical, and ecstatic.[12]

The Roman Catholic and Eastern churches typify the sacramental emphasis. The grace of God comes to man primarily through the sacraments administered by a validly ordained priesthood. Although Roman Catholic scholars would agree that the Word of God is the fundamental basis of faith and salvation, they maintain that it is through the sacramental fellowship man becomes a member of the church and a partaker of salvation. That this emphasis on the sacraments tends to enhance the position of the priest, who must have received valid orders for the administration of the Sacrament, leads to a hierarchical system and an emphasis on the church as the ultimate source of authority.

The evangelical churches tend to emphasize the preaching of the Word and the reception of the message of salvation in faith. The sacraments are of course recognized as means of grace, but since they are connected with and in a sense dependent on the Word, the proclamation of the message becomes the chief means of grace. The pulpit shares a place with the altar as the center of the service, and can even crowd the altar aside to claim the central place. The church is conceived of in terms of those who, hearing the Word, confess their faith in the biblical message of salvation and life. The minister is primarily a preacher, who has been called indeed by God through the action of the congregation which he serves.

The ecstatic sects place the emphasis on the presence and activity of the Holy Spirit. The Spirit is given to each individual as an authoritative guide for both faith and action, and a source of new powers in the believer's life. The Spirit is not bound to any historical documents or institutions, although the gift of the Spirit is connected with the preaching of the Word. This preaching may be done by anyone, without distinction.

It is, of course, true that no Christian church represents an exclusive emphasis on one or the other of these three types of answers

---

[12]See also chapter 2.

how grace is received. It is also true that in every case the Scriptures remain the source of God's revelation and the valid standard for faith and life. But there is in each case a special emphasis on one particular way the grace of God comes to man. When this emphasis becomes one-sided, it results in a conception of the church which conforms to this conception of the means of grace. Instead of recognizing that God may have many ways in which to approach man and many means whereby he can restore man to fellowship with himself, man tends to insist that the approach occurs in one particular way which must be the same for all. Thus divisions occur in the church, not necessarily because men fail to believe in salvation through Christ, but because they believe that the grace of God must be appropriated through one particular means.

Besides the means of grace as one principal cause of divisions, many other factors, both religious and secular, cause disagreements and strife, but the church could find a basis of union if it took seriously the fact that man is saved by grace alone in Christ. When Paul found divisions in the Corinthian congregation, he asked them to remember that they were saved by grace alone, and therefore none of them had anything to boast of. "What have you that you did not receive? If then you received it, why do you boast as if it were not a gift?" (I Cor. 4:7). The church is one because it is founded, established, and lives only by the grace of God.

If the church is one, it is also inclusive. It cannot be the one without the other. The command of Jesus was to make disciples of all nations: Jews and Gentiles, barbarians and Greeks, without distinction. There was a remarkable variety of people and views in the New Testament church, and they seem to have gotten along well together in spite of the differences. It was only when some seemed to deny the fundamental doctrine of salvation by grace that Paul drew the line (Gal. 1:8). The New Testament itself is indeed the chief witness to the unity of the church in its emphasis on salvation by the grace of God in Christ, as well as a witness to the diversity and variety among the Christians. It is fortunate that the

New Testament contains not only the letters of Paul, but also James, the Synoptic Gospels, John, Hebrews, and Revelation.

The church is as inclusive and catholic as the grace of God. It is the open arms of the Father welcoming the errant son; in its final form it is the kingdom into which people come from the east and the west, from the north and the south, to sit at tables with Abraham, Isaac, and Jacob, and all the redeemed of all generations.

What gives a man the right to belong to the church? That he has subscribed to some doctrinal articles, that he can answer correctly the questions in the catechism, that he has been baptized in a certain manner, or that he yields obedience to a hierachy? No, the only right he can claim is the grace of God. The only qualification that he can present for membership is that he needs God. The Bible declares that anyone who calls upon the name of the Lord shall be saved. It is not necessary to call according to a certain formula or in a prescribed pattern. The inarticulate cry of a lost and bewildered soul will be heard by him who is "the God of all grace." The church has no right to erect barriers and set limits to the grace of God. There must be nothing in its program or proclamation that obscures or denies that the grace of God is free and that salvation is for all. The entrance into the church must be as broad and wide as the grace and mercy of God.

If it should be objected that this description suggests "the wide gate and the broad way that leads to destruction," and that Jesus spoke of "the strait gate and the narrow way that leads to life," the answer to that objection, too, is found in the grace of God. The Bible insists that salvation is by grace alone. This is the true stumbling block, the *skandalon* of the biblical message, that man must acknowledge his status as a sinner who is unable to help himself, and who must trust in God's grace alone for salvation and life. Paul recognized, too, that this was "the narrow way," because this is the one demand that man refuses to meet, and the one aspect of the gospel which he is most anxious to tone down or remove. Man may be willing to give up almost anything that he has, to sacrifice some of his dearest possessions, or to endure any kind of hardship and privation—provided he can be assured that by such means he can win the favor and good will of God. He is willing to suffer anything and surrender anything except *self*. He may humble himself and crawl in the dust, but he wants credit for it both from God and men.

Such an attitude and ascetic actions carried out in this spirit are sin, because they are a form of rebellion against God who alone saves and gives life. Paul shows that such ascetic practices are of no value and that "they are really only a catering to the flesh" (Col. 2:23 A.T.). The way is narrow because it demands the death of self. "Whoever seeks to gain his life [*psyche,* "self"] will lose it, but whoever loses his life will preserve it" (Luke 17:33). Since the grace of God can be free only if there is nothing that a man can do to merit it, man must receive it without any pretense of merit or worthiness in himself. The church must exemplify in its proclamation and practices this character of the grace of God. Only so can it be *one* and *catholic.*

If the door of the church is open to all who seek the grace of God, it is also the entrance into a life of growth and sanctification. The Philippian jailer who was baptized by Paul on the simple confession of faith in Jesus would have to learn a great deal more after that experience about the significance of the new life. Over the door of the church the inscription is not only, "Come, for all is now ready," but also, "Let everyone who names the name of the Lord depart from iniquity." Easy as the entrance into the church is, it leads to a road that implies struggle and hardship. Paul was never satisfied with the present status of his converts. He gave them credit for living a life well-pleasing to God, but he wanted them to "do so more and more" (I Thess. 4:1). He thought of the congregation as a place where Christians are to grow in grace and to "increase and abound in love to one another and to all men" (I Thess. 3:12). The church is not a haven of rest: it is a place where the struggle against the powers of evil and the ancient enemy is to be carried on with all the weapons which God supplies to his people (Eph. 6:10 ff.). The Christian is free; free to live in the confidence of victory through the living Lord, and free to fight against all that would oppose God's will and purpose. The church is not made up of people who have arrived at the goal: it is a people prepared by God to serve his purposes in the world.

God's people in all ages are the ones whom he has redeemed into fellowship with himself, and we have seen that all through the Bible they have been redeemed in order to serve him. The anonymous prophet of the Exile envisioned a people who were to be a light to the Gentiles, and from whom the message of salvation was to go out into all the world. The Christians have been redeemed in order that they may fulfill God's intention for humanity: to worship him, and to be concerned for the temporal and eternal welfare of the neighbor. They have been redeemed and at the same time taken up into the context of God's plans to become his instruments for the realization of his eternal purpose.

If we have interpreted the biblical record aright, God is engaged in a ceaseless struggle to redeem his creation and to establish his kingdom. The proximate goal of the activity is the preaching of the gospel to the whole world in order that men may know God in Christ and acknowledge him as Lord and Savior. This goal is a part of our life and work, and this we can see and understand without much difficulty. The church's mission is the proclamation of salvation in Christ to the whole world.

The ultimate goal is hidden from us in the mind of God himself. Even Jesus declared, of that day and that hour no one knows except the Father (Matt. 24:36). How, when, and where that goal will be reached, God has not revealed to us, but he has given us a promise of a new event which will be greater and more marvelous than anything that has gone before, because it will involve the fulfillment of all his promises. Even though we do not know how his purpose will be achieved, we are confident that God will continue his gracious redemptive activity to the very end. Just as God has disclosed himself in every one of the biblical events as Redeemer and Savior, so the last event will bring redemption and life to his people. "When these things begin to take place, look up and raise your heads, because your redemption is drawing near" (Luke 21:28). The whole activity of God in judgment and redemption looks forward to the ultimate goal of the establishment of the eternal kingdom of God.

# Indexes

# INDEX OF PERSONS AND SUBJECTS

# INDEX OF SCRIPTURE PASSAGES

32:21, 22 — 80      *Jonah*              *Zechariah*
*Amos*              4:11 — 48           13:7 — 68
2:4 — 76            *Micah*              *Malachi*
9:7 — 48            4:1, 2 — 43          1:11 — 44
                                         3:1 — 68

## NEW TESTAMENT

*Matthew*               28:18 — 86, 134         4:18 — 116, 121
1:18 — 105              28:19 — 37              4:18, 19 — 110, 163
1:22 — 69              28:20 — 23              4:21 — 69
2:5 — 69               *Mark*                   9:24 — 32
2:15, 23 — 64, 69      1:2, 3 — 68             10:11 — 93
3:3 — 69               1:10, 11 — 109          11:20 — 93, 112
4:14 — 69              1:14, 15 — 59           11:21, 22 — 121
5:17 — 39, 75, 78      1:15 — 73               16:17 — 75, 78
5:18 — 78              2:22 — 38               17:33 — 188
5:21 — 172             2:23-28 — 150           18:31 — 61
5:23, 24 — 151         3:14 — 45               21:16-18 — 100
5:48 — 172             4:12 — 68               21:28 — 87, 190
6:2 — 148              6:38 — 108              24:2 f. — 131
6:12, 14 — 173         7:6 — 68                24:25, 27 — 61
7:11 — 163             7:9-13 — 150 f.         24:44, 45 — 61
8:16 — 12              8:31, 33 — 53, 80       *John*
8:17 — 69              9:9, 10 — 80, 132       1:1-3 — 12, 103
11:10 — 69             9:31 — 80               1:13 — 103
11:19 — 179            10:35 — 53              1:14 — 13
11:28 — 168            10:33 — 80              1:17 — 38
13:14, 15 — 69         10:43, 44 — 181         1:23 — 69
13:35 — 69             10:45 — 80, 121         1:29 — 116
16:16 — 60             12:10, 36 — 68          2:1-11 — 37, 109
16:22 — 80             14:27 — 68              2:17 — 69
18:20 — 176            14:49 — 61              2:22 — 65
21:4 — 69              15:28 — 68              3:17 — 69
21:33 — 103            16:4 — 131              3:34 — 111
22:40 — 155            *Luke*                   5:19, 30, 36 — 109
22:37-40 — 145         1:26 ff. — 104          5:21, 22 — 34
24:14 — 40             1:32, 33 — 104          5:21 — 135
24:36 — 108, 189       1:35 — 104              5:39 — 61
25:41 — 34             1:46-55 — 25, 105       6:38 — 109
26:54, 56 — 69         1:68-79 — 105           6:31, 45 — 69
27:9 — 69              2:52 — 107              7:3, 16 — 109
28:2 — 131             3:23 — 105              7:39 — 178

*Type used in this book*
Body, 11 on 13 Garamond
Display, Lydian
Paper: "R" Standard White Antique